MONOTASKING

How to Focus Your Mind, Be More Productive, and Improve Your Brain Health

Staffan Nöteberg

Racehorse Publishing

Raise your head to see the way, lower your head to do the job.
~ Chinese idiom

CONTENTS

PREFACE

PERSONAL PRODUCTIVITY SYSTEMS HELP us to manage our personal time in the most efficient, productive, and effective way. However, systems that are too complicated, too rigid, or too time consuming will sooner or later be rejected—no matter how much potential they have to help us.

Rigid personal productivity systems are often developed by engineers who normally program computers. Even though they try to specify in detail how we should act in every possible scenario, they won't be able to describe most situations. The world is too complex for rule-based systems. A better approach is to replace the rules with good practices. Then human intuition can come to the rescue.

Complicated personal productivity systems are created by personal productivity gurus. They love to have a multitude of lists, protocols, and tools. But if inventing personal productivity systems isn't your profession, then you'll want an easy system that can be implemented promptly and can rapidly result in productive habits.

Time-consuming personal productivity systems are usually implemented in your organization by management consultants. They persuade top management that employees are lazy and accordingly must constantly report upwards. These systems tend to consume more resources than they free up.

Monotasking is a powerful system based on switching between prioritizing and focusing. It's flexible, easy to learn, and minimally time consuming. However, it is still very capable—and fun. It also embraces the ability to evolve. You can start with this textbook version and then adapt it to your circumstances when you find that you would benefit from that.

This book is organized in seven chapters. The first provides an overview of the monotasking method, and the remaining chapters cover the six areas in which it is most important to achieve success in order to be productive:

- Cut down on tasks to do
- Focus on one task now
- Never procrastinate
- Progress incrementally
- Simplify cooperation
- Recharge creative thinking

The chapters are independent and can be read in whatever order you like. However, if you want to succeed with the monotasking method, you should understand all of them. My recommendation is to use the "panorama cue" while reading this book. It will give you a good idea of how you want to customize monotasking to your special circumstances.

I hope you'll enjoy the book and benefit from monotasking!

// Staffan

INTRODUCTION
THE FIVE AXIOMS OF MONOTASKING

LITTLE DID THE YOUNG and curious psychology researcher Bluma Zeigarnik know that her seemingly trivial observation in a café would change the game of personal productivity. This was back in the 1920s, but today we are still struggling with how to best use her findings in the modern environment of office work.

Bluma was fascinated by a waiter's ability to remember what everyone had ordered when someone called for the bill. It didn't matter that Bluma's friends had spent hours in the café, ordering multiple times. The waiter successfully recalled everything.

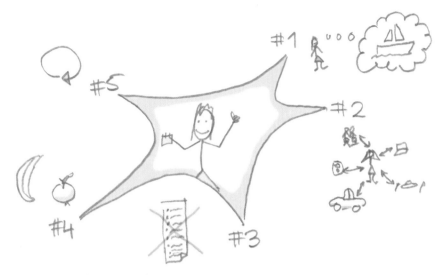

Then, half an hour after paying, they asked the waiter to rewrite the check. He couldn't. The surprising answer was, *"I can't recall what you ordered, since you've paid the bill."* Until the order was paid, it was available in detail in the waiter's memory. After that, it was forgotten.[1]

Could Bluma confirm her theory in a scientific experiment? She let 164 people know that they would perform about twenty tasks. What she didn't tell them was that half of the tasks would be interrupted before they could be completed. The tasks were interrupted in such a way that no one could suspect that the interruptions were a deliberate part of the experiment. Some tasks were manual work, such as constructing a box of cardboard or making clay figures. Others were mental problems, such as puzzles and arithmetic. Following the last task, participants were asked to recall the tasks they had worked on. Bluma's initial hypothesis from the café was proven correct. Approximately twice as many of the unfinished tasks were remembered compared to the completed ones.[2]

The fact that we remember unfinished or incomplete tasks better than the completed tasks usually goes under the name *Zeigarnik effect*. In order to remember it better, I prefer to call it *the waiter effect*. As we'll see later in this book, it can cause us problems. But we can also use it to our advantage. For example, leaving the office in the middle of a task helps you get started easily the next morning, eliminating some of that before-lunch procrastination. This leads us to the first axiom:

- **Axiom #1:** Started tasks will unconditionally demand space in our daily thinking until we either complete them or delete them.

Every time we switch from one task to another, our brain's executive control does two things. First, it activates the goal shifting: I did this, now I'll do that. Second, it creates the context for the new task. The latter is called *rule activation*.

Switching tasks consumes time. One switch can take as little as a tenth of a second, but during a day of constant switching, it might consume a significant part of your productive time. While looking productive, you're actually wasting a good amount of time between tasks.[3]

Task switching also induces errors. Clearing the working memory and reloading the rules of the current task over and over isn't the best foundation for problem solving. The more complex your task, the more errors will arise because of task switching.

Repeated task switching also reduces what is popularly known as emotional intelligence, or EQ. The switching leads to anxiety, which in turn raises levels of the stress hormone cortisol in the brain. This may contribute to aggressive and impulsive behavior.

Finally, task switching is energy intensive. It burns up oxygenated glucose in the brain. Unfortunately, that is exactly the fuel we need to stay on a task. Task switching thus initiates a vicious cycle, increasing the risk of even more task switching. Depleting these resources also makes us feel exhausted, and even disoriented, quite quickly.[4] Here's the second axiom:

- **Axiom #2:** Task switching not only slows us down but also inevitably depletes our brain energy.

In our modern society, many things are changing all the time. The task that used to be the most important may no longer be so. It might be that the task requires much more time than we originally predicted, or you might have discovered or been given another new and even more important task. At least once an hour, we should ask ourselves Lakein's question: *"What's the best use of my time right now?"*[5]

Even though prioritizing tasks demands significant energy from the brain, we must nevertheless do it often. By limiting the options to only those few which can reasonably be most important, we make it easier for the brain. The monotasking method provides many simple and effective practices and tools, such as the *panorama session* and the *short list*, for doing this. It conserves available brain energy and puts it to better use.

Everyone has more tasks on their mental list than they'll have time to perform. Prioritizing is about doing the first things first. It's not about prioritizing based on urgency or how long the task has been waiting for your attention. Neither is it following outdated plans.

Transparency is critical when our planning is this dynamic. Stakeholders are waiting for results. They have the right to be informed frequently about whether we intend to carry out this task now or later or not at all. The third axiom thus regards our responsibility:

- **Axiom #3:** We are responsible for prioritizing the number one most important task right now, as we can always come up with an almost infinite number of valuable tasks to work on.

Brief breaks every hour help us to focus. Our attention span is limited. If we work on the same task for several hours without a break, our minds start to wander. Breaks will also set our muscles in motion. Eight hours of sedentary work every day isn't good for anyone.[6] In addition when we disconnect from our task during breaks, we'll get new insights—that's creative thinking. Finally, breaks are a natural point in time for eventually re-prioritizing which task is currently the most important one.

The National Highway Traffic Safety Administration estimates that more than 100,000 people are killed or injured in the United States in sleep- or drowsiness-related traffic crashes every year.[7] There's consensus among scientific researchers that lack of sleep and low sleep quality increases the number of errors we make daily in the office reducing our productivity. In addition, when we forgo the important REM stage of sleep, we miss opportunities to learn by experience. There are many resources out there for tips and methods for improving your sleep.

Physical exercise is one proven method of improving sleep.[8] Exercising also increases our health and reduces the risk of age-related cognitive decline.[9] Creative thinking increases when we exercise.[10] Something as simple as having a discussion meeting during a walk instead of in a conference room can do wonders for generating new approaches.[11] We are also able to think better when our brains are oxygenated.

Brain energy isn't only affected by sleep and exercising. What we put in our mouth makes a difference. Almost everything we eat is converted into glucose, which, as mentioned above, is the brain's fuel. Working on an empty stomach lowers productivity. Pasta, bread, and soft drinks all release glucose rapidly, but this leads to quick bursts of energy followed by steep declines. High-fat foods consumed in combination with complex carbs, like whole grains, provide more sustained energy that won't result in the blood sugar spikes and drops that can negatively affect the brain. A diet rich in fruits and vegetables can positively affect our mood, making us happier.[12] A nourishing and diverse diet is thus fundamental for productivity in the short term as well as in the long term. All these things together form the fourth axiom:

- **Axiom #4:** Taking breaks, sleeping well, exercising, and eating healthy are mandatory investments, if we want to maintain a sustainable pace every day.

As modern office workers, we find ourselves in the midst of a complex system undergoing constant change. The market for the services our employer offers changes. Our mission changes. Our individual roles and responsibilities change. We learn new things and become both more skilled and effective. Colleagues quit and others are hired, triggering new group dynamics in our team.

There are no methods that work best for everyone. We are all different. We think differently. We are motivated by different things. Despite this, we can learn from each other and experiment with methods that others have found useful.

Peter Drucker said in 1954 that the only valid definition of a business purpose is to create a customer.[13] As individuals, we need to ask ourselves why we are here. How can we help our employer solve our customers' problems? To be faster and more efficient is not enough—we also need to be more effective.

Finally, it can be fun to improve our daily practices. Mastery is one of the most powerful human drives.[14] When we feel like we're growing and become more proficient in what we do, we become more committed to our work and more satisfied with the outcomes.

We must challenge the status quo on a daily basis. Thus, the final axiom:

- **Axiom #5:** We must adapt our method to our own circumstances individually, gradually, and based on our recent personal experiences. There is no one-size-fits-all method.

To recap, these are the five axioms: (1) starting makes us want to finish, (2) multitasking decreases our speed and energy, (3) it's our responsibility to prioritize on importance rather than on urgency, (4) breaks, sleep, and a healthy lifestyle are all mandatory to maintaining a sustainable pace, and (5) embracing change and continuous improvement is critical in our ever changing world. These five axioms form the foundation of the monotasking productivity system.

CHAPTER 1
MONOTASKING IN A NUTSHELL

"NO. YOU'VE GOT IT wrong, Mike. Everything you didn't circle just became your Avoid-At-All-Cost list." That's what the incomparably successful investor Warren Buffett told his pilot, Mike Flint, to do with every task that didn't make it into his list of his top five most important goals.[15]

We can choose to be more effective. We can stop starting so many new tasks and start completing the tasks we have committed to. We can prioritize the most important tasks instead of those that are most urgent. And we can put our focus on one task at a time.

This first chapter of this book is an introduction to monotasking. It describes the problems and challenges we face in trying to be productive in our modern busy lives. It also presents some of the monotasking tools that make us effective, such as the *short list*, *jumbled priorities,* and the *panorama cue*.

IN ONE MINUTE: THE MONOTASKING METHOD

Five simple concepts:

- **The short list** is your epicenter in the monotasking method. It holds a maximum of five of your tasks, those that are most important right now. You can only add a task to this list if you remove another.
- **The monotasking session** is focused on one single task from your short list. The session is terminated by the panorama cue.
- **The panorama cue** is an alarm set to the next vertical position of the minute hand (9:00, 9:30, 10:00, etc.) that is at least twenty-five minutes away. It transfers your focus from the monotasking session to the panorama session.
- **The panorama session** is a time to look at all your potential tasks and ask Lakein's question: *"What's the best use of my time right now?"*
- **Jumbled priorities** should be avoided. Prioritizing urgent tasks over important tasks is an example of jumbled priorities. Completing our most important tasks makes our long-term goals come true.

Questionnaire:

In order to kickstart your neurons, put a checkmark next to every statement below that you consider to be a recurring time robber in your current workplace:

- ☐ Task switching
- ☐ Too many stakeholders
- ☐ Urgent tasks
- ☐ Three-hour meetings without breaks
- ☐ Uninspiring mornings
- ☐ Noisy colleagues
- ☐ Incomplete work
- ☐ Everyday administration
- ☐ Long-term planning
- ☐ Hard-to-find information
- ☐ High responsibility and low authority

- ☐ Impromptu tasks
- ☐ Delayed decisions
- ☐ Fear of opposing management
- ☐ Lack of privacy
- ☐ Lack of exercise facilities
- ☐ Blame games
- ☐ Perfection desire
- ☐ Going from one crisis to another
- ☐ Emerging deadlines

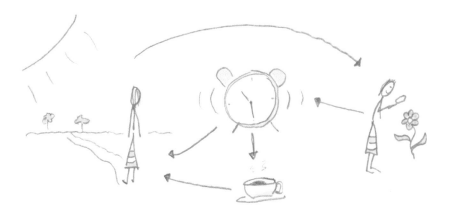

MONOTASKING AND PANORAMA RHYTHM

Off the top of your head, write down important tasks on your short list. Go ahead, I'll wait. After throwing a glance at yesterday's list, you might add more, but never reuse yesterday's list carelessly. Copied tasks must still be important. Limit the number of tasks to a maximum of five.

You switch between panorama mode and monotasking during the day. When you feel like it, you can take breaks in between. Monotasking means zooming in on one and only one task. Panorama means seeing the bigger picture and choosing the most important task for right now.

The monotasking session always starts with setting an alarm: this is the panorama cue. Set it to the next vertical position of the minute hand of the clock, or the one after if it is less than twenty-five minutes away: If the time is 9:15, you set the alarm to 10:00; if the time is 11:03, you set the alarm to 11:30.

When new task ideas emerge in your brain, just jot them down on the short list instead of switching tasks immediately. When people interrupt you, ask them if you can delay your contribution. Of course, do help them if their task is more important than yours.

Put a small "x" next to the chosen task on the short list before switching from panorama mode to monotasking. There must be no doubt about what task or goal you have committed to spend your attention on during the monotasking session. Cross out completed tasks on your list as you go along.

JUMBLED PRIORITIES

"I have two kinds of problems, the urgent and the important. The urgent are not important, and the important are never urgent." This food for thought from 1954 is the foundation for the Eisenhower Box, named after the 34th president of the United States.[16]

Here's an example. My coworkers urged me to prepare a cake for the coffee break this afternoon—it's urgent. But urgent does not equal important. The sales report has a deadline next week. It's less urgent (immediate), but it's much more important. Important tasks are never urgent. So, write the sales report and forget about the cake.

In 1967, Charles E. Hummel used irony when he wrote: *"Urgent, though less important, tasks call for immediate response—endless demands of pressure every waking hour."* He labeled this the problem of *jumbled priorities*.[17] Prioritizing urgent tasks and goals over important tasks and goals is jumbling your priorities.

Important tasks contribute to our long-term goals, while urgent tasks require instant attention. We're performing important tasks when we act in responsive mode and performing urgent tasks when we act in reactive mode. Prioritizing urgent over important is also known as *firefighting*.

Once you've determined which tasks fall into which category, which we'll talk about later, you'll need to follow through with what you've prioritized. Stephen R. Covey's third habit of highly effective people puts this very simply: Put first things first.[18] The more time you spend on urgent things, the more the pile of urgent work will grow. Other tasks that used to be important but not urgent will then become urgent as well.

"I DON'T HAVE TIME" IS A LIE

We're all aware of more tasks than we'll have time to perform. Most of these tasks are certainly possible, if we give them top priority. We get twenty-four new hours every day. The reason to say *"no"* isn't lack of time—it's the fact that other tasks have higher priority. So, stop saying, *"I don't have time."*

Well, there is one exception. If I am asked if I can solve seven hundred extra hard Sudoku puzzles tonight, I must admit that there isn't enough time, due to simple mathematics. Each Sudoku demands thirty minutes. Even if I skip dinner, television, and family—and even book reading—one night is not enough time.

But go ahead and ask me if I can solve seven hundred extra hard Sudoku puzzles in the next year. I would have to dedicate one hour each day to this task. As much as I like Sudoku, there are other, more important tasks that would be left undone. I do have time, but I choose to give higher priority to other tasks.

Why didn't I set a higher priority to fixing the hole in my wallet? Then I would still have my cash by now. When we don't prioritize our most important tasks, we spend our time on waste. If you take a peek behind *"I don't have time"* you might find a *"tyranny of the urgent."*[19]

It's how you choose to spend your time that defines your priorities. Don't feel ashamed of your priorities. By being transparent and allowing others to challenge your priorities, they'll also respect and accept your *"no."* Don't ever say, *"I don't have time."*

PANORAMA CUE

Alan Lakein suggested in the 1970s that we could use a timer while focusing.[20] The monotasking method switches between what I call the *panorama mode*—or looking at the big picture—and the *monotasking mode*. We set an alarm—the *panorama cue*—before starting the monotasking session. The cue reminds us to stop and re-assess our priorities.

The panorama cue helps us get into the flow. The alarm is set and until it goes off, we don't question whether this is the right task to do. We selected it, and now we focus 100 percent on this task—we monotask—until the alarm goes off. Then we view all potential tasks, i.e., view the panorama, and select the most important one.

Having focus sessions of a fixed length can be good for rhythm, but unfortunately, that's a structure that is usually too inflexible. Often, we have a deadline for the task we're focusing on. The time is 9:08 and we need to be at a meeting at 9:30. The obvious choice is to set the panorama cue to 9:30 or a minute or two before that.

Meetings and other *hardscape* events—i.e., commitments we can't shift—conventionally start at one of 48 moments in the day (if you're using military time): 00:00, 00:30, 01:00, 01:30, and so on through 23:30. Setting your panorama cue to the next such point in time is therefore advisable, so you don't miss the next meeting.

However, if we're not missing the start time of the next meeting, we want at least 25 minutes for monotasking mode. Example: If the time is 09:03, we set panorama cue to 9:30; if the time is 9:12, we put the panorama cue to 10:00, if the time is 10:28, we set the panorama cue to 11:00.

MONOTASKING METHOD – SUMMARY

Q: Can you give me a short description of the monotasking method?
A: Ask yourself this question: *"What's the best use of my time right now?"* Write down a maximum of five tasks that answer this question. Set your panorama cue to the next half or full hour. Select the most important task on your list and start to work, focusing solely on that task. When the alarm goes off, either take a brief break or start over, reviewing your tasks in panorama mode.

Q: And what's the elevator pitch then?
A: For people who can imagine more than one single task to do right now, monotasking is a personal productivity method that helps you complete the most important task. Unlike many other productivity methods, monotasking is easy to use, intuitive, and based on scientific research.

Q: Can everyone benefit from monotasking?
A: There are people who are not empowered to do any prioritizing. They are told to always follow detailed instructions from their superiors. These people unfortunately probably can't benefit from the monotasking method with regard to their work, but the monotasking method can be applied to personal goals as well.

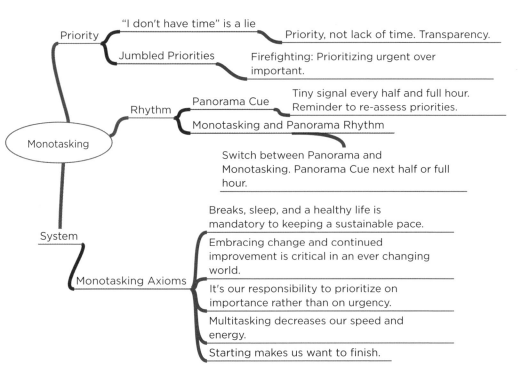

Priority

"I don't have time" is a lie

Priority, not lack of time. Transparency.

Jumbled Priorities

Firefighting: Prioritizing urgent over important.

Rhythm

Panorama Cue

Tiny signal every half and full hour. Reminder to re-assess priorities.

Monotasking and Panorama Rhythm

Monotasking

Switch between Panorama and Monotasking. Panorama Cue next half or full hour.

System

Breaks, sleep, and a healthy life is mandatory to keeping a sustainable pace.

Embracing change and continued improvement is critical in an ever changing world.

Monotasking Axioms

It's our responsibility to prioritize on importance rather than on urgency.

Multitasking decreases our speed and energy.

Starting makes us want to finish.

CHAPTER 2
CUT DOWN ON TASKS TO DO

UNCLEAR PRIORITIES ARE A major threat to productivity. We work a little bit here and we work a little bit there, but nothing is completed. The effort we put into a task may be worthless if the task is not completed. Priorities won't be clear when we have too many tasks to choose from.

We must learn to regularly remove tasks from our to-do list. To get to the root of the problem, we should also stop listening to task sources that only give us the kind of tasks we won't do anyway.

This chapter presents hands-on methods to address this problem, including the *short list* and *weeding*. These tools emphasize that we must prioritize importance, not urgency. This chapter also gives tips on how we can free up energy by reducing the influx of tasks, sometimes by saying *"no"* from the very beginning.

IN ONE MINUTE: HOW TO CUT DOWN ON TASKS TO DO

Five simple concepts:

- **The busyness fallacy** is the inadequate belief that the more tasks you engage in, the more value you add. If you totally fill your schedule up front, you won't be able to take on new and unforeseen important tasks. You will also most certainly become a bottleneck for others.
- **The short list** is the list of your five most important tasks right now. You write them down on paper every morning. You're only allowed to add a new task to the short list if you cross out another task, whether the crossed-out task is completed or not.
- **Weekly purpose** lets you focus on *why*. Write an improvement, property, or quality on an index card. It should be something you really want to deliver this week. Attach the card to your cubicle wall. Whenever in doubt, you'll be reminded of the purpose of this week.
- **The grass catcher list** is the unsorted collection of tasks and ideas you haven't yet refused but won't do right now. Write down three things for each item that you add to the list: the goal, the stakeholder, and the date it entered the list.
- **Weeding** is the weekly act of removing tasks from the grass catcher list. Weeding is a necessary process for keeping the list readable, timely, and trustworthy. You add new tasks spontaneously to the grass catcher, but you clean this list in one weekly batch.

Questionnaire:

In order to kickstart your neurons, put a checkmark next to every statement below that you consider to be a recurring time robber in your current workplace:

- ☐ Too many concurrent projects
- ☐ Too many stakeholders
- ☐ Too many electronic messages received
- ☐ Boss can't take no for an answer
- ☐ Fear of stopping projects
- ☐ Impromptu tasks
- ☐ Incomplete work
- ☐ Non-authorized decision meetings
- ☐ Vague purpose

- ☐ Short-term results desired
- ☐ Long lead time
- ☐ Sisyphean paperwork
- ☐ Constant pressure
- ☐ Unreliable colleagues
- ☐ Changing requirements
- ☐ Lack of commitment from technical experts
- ☐ Workload grows faster than capacity
- ☐ Lack of delegation
- ☐ Management by crisis
- ☐ No priorities

A CUCUMBER AND AN ARTICHOKE MEET OUTSIDE A BRICK-AND-MORTAR SHOP

Cucumber: Good to see you, Artie. How are things?

Artichoke: They're great, thank you. I have important roles in eight different projects. In addition, I engage in some personal tasks that are important for the company's future.

Cucumber: If you participate in so many things, there must be many grateful stakeholders out there!

Artichoke: Well, all eight projects have different project managers. Each of them wants me to work with their particular things. Also, I'd prefer to spend time on my own projects.

Cucumber: You mean that you have become the bottleneck of the company?

Artichoke: Yes, indeed. Although I work late nights, I never have time to deliver before deadline. That holds my colleagues up from completing their own work.

Cucumber: How are you holding them up?

Artichoke: They can't continue until they get my delivery. They are waiting for me.

Cucumber: Do you know John Little?[21]

Artichoke: John who?

Cucumber: I think you would deliver quicker if you started fewer tasks.

Artichoke: You mean that I must stop starting and start finishing?

Cucumber: Yes. Select the most important project. Tell the seven other project managers that they have lower priority. Some of those will choose someone else who has more time to work for them. It's best for everyone.

Artichoke: That sounds good. My new policy should be to have a short queue of pending projects, say *"no"* to new stuff, and share that priority with everyone.

THE BUSYNESS FALLACY

Being busy typically has one of two sources: it is either our procrastination strategy or the result of our inability to organize our lives well. Busy people are perceived as important. They even feel they are important. But busy isn't the same as productive. A 100 percent full workload leaves us with no time to take on new important tasks.

During a psychological experiment, people who were asked to calculate their hourly wage before listening to a short piece of music were more impatient while the music was playing.[22] They wanted to do something more profitable. This is a sign of our times, that it's a widening gap between what we can do and what we're doing now in this moment.

Tim Ferriss wrote facetiously that the options are almost limitless for creating busyness.[23] Why not commit yourself to producing large quantities of documents? Or aspire for key roles in all ongoing projects? Or, above all, be a link in as many chains of command as possible?

Busyness fills our calendar with meetings and other commitments we can't shift. Thus, we can never deliver what we committed to at those meetings. It also overloads our cognitive capacity. When we're overly busy and tasks become urgent, the fight-or-flight mode will kick in, crowding out our analytical proficiency. Priorities become inflexible.

Idleness is, paradoxically, necessary to getting any work done. You'll see the wholeness and make unexpected connections.[24] Also, replacing unpredictable deadlines with timeboxing makes you more adaptable to change. A good start is to never use the word *busy* as an answer to your stakeholders.

WEEKLY PURPOSE

We are able to find the highest levels of motivation when we find purpose in our work.[25] Purpose often comes from understanding that what you're doing in this very minute is a part of something bigger and very useful. The monotasking method helps you figure out your purpose for the upcoming week. Here's the how-to:

1. List all of your current and upcoming projects, not just small tasks.
2. For each project, write a realistic improvement that you could make within one week, if you allowed yourself to focus on this particular project, starting today. Think of the improvement as a property or quality that is not present right now. For example: calling a hundred potential customers, writing that sales report and distributing it to all stakeholders, or completing performance appraisals with all subordinates.
3. Write the ONE most important improvement from among the improvements you discovered in the second step in the center of an index card or any smallish piece of paper. Write with a broad pen or marker. Add the date of the day one week from today in the top right corner. This is the imagined delivery date.
4. Attach the card to your cubicle wall so that you'll see it every time you lift your eyes from the computer screen.

This doesn't mean that you will spend 100 percent of your time on this single task. But, whenever in doubt, you'll be reminded of the purpose of this week.

THE SHORT LIST

Every entry in a to-do list comes with a sense of urgency by its very presence on the list. The traditional everything-in-life to-do list is often long and sometimes partly outdated. With so many tasks crying out for action, we feel overwhelmed. Often, this feeling of overwhelm prevents us from acting.

Limiting your to-do list to five tasks is a great way to become more productive. And it doesn't hurt if your list is even shorter. However, if a new important task comes in, you must trade away one of the old entries. Trading away means striking it off. The removed task might re-enter later when there's more room, but the list can't be longer than five tasks.

Tasks on the short list should be small and actionable. A small task is one that is estimated to take no more than an hour to complete. Obviously, many tasks take much longer than an hour to complete, so break down those big tasks into smaller sub-tasks. Actionable tasks describe outcomes: for instance, "complete report," "outline report," or "schedule meeting."

Some tasks are perceived as important day after day. But for some reason we don't touch them. They are doomed to be the eternal runners-up. Since this type of task is basically noise, it shouldn't be on the short list. Make a fresh list every morning; don't reuse the one from yesterday.

The short list is an essential building block in the monotasking method. Every morning you write down a maximum of five small, actionable tasks. When you complete one, you cross it out. If adding something makes the list exceed five tasks, then some other task is taken away.

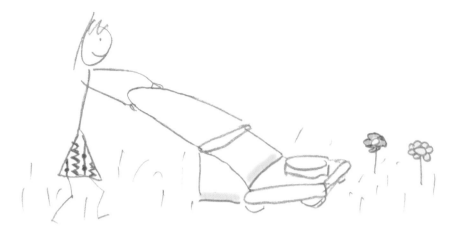

GRASS CATCHER LIST

"Hey, if you've got some spare time, can you do me a favor? I've written this report and it would be nice to have a second opinion. I'd love it if you could take a look at it." Your colleague dropped a low priority task on you, which you might act on later. Where should you put this information for now?

Tasks you're not acting on immediately are like the mix of dandelions, grass, and other weeds caught by the grass catcher when you mow the lawn—it's all fed to the rabbits. They accept some of it and reject the rest of it. These tasks are collected in the *grass catcher list*.[26]

The *short list* is limited to a maximum of five of your top priority tasks and it's written today, while the grass catcher isn't limited at all, and neither is it prioritized. You only add to it now and then. It's just a collection of ideas that you don't want to forget, but that you're not acting on right now.

When you add to the grass catcher list, three fields are mandatory: the goal (of course), the stakeholder, and the date it entered the list. The latter is used when trimming the list. The oldest tasks must leave. Being prioritization runner-up for a long time proves that this task will likely never be done.

The grass catcher has an important role: it helps you remember tasks you can't do right now but that might still become top priorities in the future. However, most tasks in this list are simply noise. They are tasks that arguably add some value but not enough to ever win the prioritization race.

WEEDING

By now you should have a *short list*, containing the five most important tasks right now, and the *grass catcher list*, containing the rest of the tasks that don't qualify for the short list right now. However, the grass catcher list is always at risk of becoming too long.

Weeding is the systematic removal of tasks from the grass catcher list. It's a necessary process for keeping the list readable, timely, and trustworthy. Otherwise, we'll sooner or later ignore the almost endless list of tasks that we at some point in the past wanted to do.

Weed the grass catcher list once a week, or whenever it grows too long. Copy a maximum of five tasks to a new grass catcher list and shred the old one. The selection criterion is the importance of the task. Save the most important—not the most urgent—tasks for the new list.

This is where those three mandatory fields for every grass catcher item come into play: the goal, the stakeholder, and the date it entered the list. That date is hinting at something. Tasks that seem extremely important but have been stuck in the grass catcher list for a long time are probably not important.

During the week, we may add and add an unlimited number of tasks to the grass catcher list, but once a week, weeding kicks in and makes the list usable again. This is also a perfect opportunity to check in and make sure that our weekly purpose is aligned with our grass catcher list.

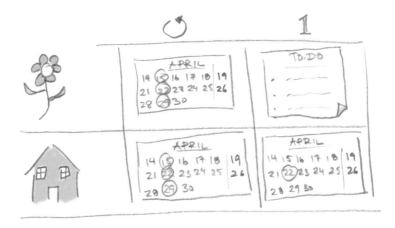

HARDSCAPE AND SOFTSCAPE

In the context of landscape management, softscape refers to living elements like flowerbeds, gardens, and trees. Inanimate materials incorporated into the landscape, like stone, driveways, and walls are called hardscape. Landscape masterpieces balance hardscape and softscape in harmony.

In the monotasking productivity system, *hardscape* is a term used to indicate tasks that are bound to be executed at a certain time. They are usually externally committed, like meetings, appointments, and events. Hardscape tasks must be in your calendar or else you may forget about them.

Tasks you can decide yourself when to execute are accordingly *softscape*. Recurring softscape tasks can be scheduled in your calendar. But softscape tasks that need to be done only once live in your short list or your grass catcher list. These tasks are executed during your discretionary time.

For instance, if you decide to clean your desk every Wednesday, it's a recurring task. It's not externally committed, and it can be deferred to Thursday one week without notifying anyone. Schedule such recurring softscape tasks in your calendar.

It's speculative in a negative way to put softscape tasks you do just once in your calendar. Something more important may show up and spoil your whole schedule. Instead, you schedule general discretionary time. Prioritizing—done during your *panorama mode*—is then based on your most recent knowledge.

DISCRETIONARY TIME FAMINE

Most office workers have discretionary time and non-discretionary time.[27] Together, they occupy 100 percent of our office time. We need to find a balance between them, so that neither of them starve.

Discretionary time is when we can choose what to do. This is typically when we sit at our desks, picking tasks and executing them. Within the responsibilities our employer assigns to us, we're empowered to manage this time. Personal productivity is for discretionary time.

Non-discretionary time—sometimes called *imposed time*[28]—is locked. We can't control what we're doing. Non-discretionary time includes meetings, lunches, or serving people. If you work in first line support, all your time might be non-discretionary.

A symptom of imbalance is that the tasks you're responsible for don't progress at the speed you and others expect them to. In that case, you have two options: either negotiate away some of your responsibilities or else expand and protect your discretionary time.

Non-discretionary time tends to be scheduled in our calendar. Discretionary time can be there too. Try to block out hours for discretionary time. Don't decide upfront how to spend these hours, just make sure they are free from appointments.

MONOTASKING TOOLS

Throughout this book, I try to be agnostic about what tools to use. My advice is to use the simplest tools you can find that work for you. Start simple and expand when you reach—not just predict—limitations. Below are some more general topics to think about.

You'll easily find feature-rich monotasking productivity apps. Keeping the short list online makes it accessible everywhere. On the other hand, pen and paper have more degrees of freedom. Any time you want, you may introduce new symbols or rules on your sheet.

Jim Benson calls his very hands-on method *Personal Kanban.* Inspired by Lean principles from manufacturing, it visualizes tasks with sticky notes that are pulled from left to right on a physical board.[29] In monotasking terms, our short list is a backlog and our work in progress is limited to one task.

Sometimes you might create multiple task lists, perhaps for different projects. David Allen suggests context-based lists. Each list has a theme: either the tool or the location or the situation needed to complete it.[30] Unfortunately, having multiple lists often handicaps our ability to prioritize. Is Task List 1 more important right now than Task List 2? Or vice-versa?

The most general advice is: if it isn't broken, don't fix it. We just need a place to jot down the names of the top five tasks from our short list. We want to be able to remove or add tasks in the easiest possible way. Features like long-term storage and mass distribution are of no benefit, since the monotasking method is a tool for personal, medium- and short-term prioritization and immediate action.

HEALTHY AMOUNT OF RECEIVED MESSAGES

Emails are a common source of tasks, most of which probably belong on your grass catcher list. However, when you return from a week's holiday to find 687 new emails in your inbox, there's probably some important information hidden in there. But how can you possibly find it? You must put yourself back in charge of the flow of information into your inbox. Push will be replaced by pull.

Start by unsubscribing from all the electronic mailing lists you haven't read in the past month. Use the same strategy with newsletters from commercial companies. If this feels scary, you can schedule a session every week to browse the web-based archive behind the emails and newsletters.

Set up a private email account if you don't already have one. Never register your professional mail address with social media or other services that are irrelevant to your professional work. As a bonus, the amount of spam received in your work inbox will be heavily reduced.

Set up your email client to automatically sort messages from work-related systems into folders with the same name as the systems they're sent from. Also, calibrate the settings in these systems so that you only receive notifications relevant to you—that is, as few as possible.

Studies have found that after seeing an email notification it takes more than a minute to recover to the speed at which you were working previously.[31] Here's a rule of thumb: decrease the number of received messages per day by ten and you'll save one workweek per year.

INBOX AS KITCHEN SINK OR BOOKSHELF?

Do you manage your email inbox like a kitchen sink or like a bookshelf? The answer won't only enable or disable your ability to practice *Inbox Zero*—the habit of regularly processing your inbox to empty[32]—it'll also put you in either cognitive exhausted or cognitive alert mode.

You bought a new book and read it. Now you want to put it on your bookshelf, which, unfortunately, happens to be full. You skim the spines and almost randomly remove one book to make room for your new book. The bookshelf is left unsorted. Do you recognize this? Probably.

Your kitchen sink is full of a combination of leftovers, dirty dishes, and plastic packaging materials. You glance at it and decide to systematically remove the cucumber pieces and leave everything else in the same messy state as you found it. Do you recognize this? Absolutely not.

Understanding, deciding, recalling, memorizing, and *inhibiting* are the five functions that make up the majority of our conscious thoughts. These functions are intensive consumers of glucose and oxygen in our brains, and overuse makes us feel exhausted.[33] Managing the inbox as a bookshelf relies on all five.

Kitchen sink cleaning is not completed until everything is removed. Every single email must be deleted, archived, or put in a to-do folder. Inbox zero is not a continuous state. Analogous to cleaning out the kitchen sink, we ought to do it two or three times a day.

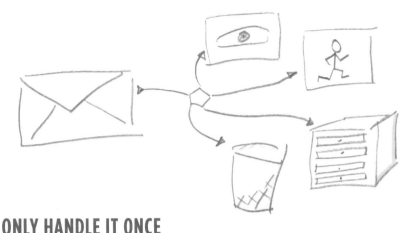

ONLY HANDLE IT ONCE

Email clients and text messaging apps are examples of inboxes that receive electronic messages. In the same way, our paper mailbox is an inbox. Even our memory is an inbox, and the parts of our brain that are responsible for creativity are an inbox where new ideas are born. Think of your inbox as the reception area of a company.

The receptionist registers visitors in the system; she doesn't solve their problems. She also helps people who unfortunately went to the wrong address. Until she has registered a visitor, he's stuck in a buffer and can never get help, no matter how important his case is.

We can sort and move messages into several different bucket types. This applies whether the inbox is our memory, an electronic message client, or a physical mailbox. One of these buckets is obviously the trash can. Here, we throw messages we know we won't need in the future.

We should also have an unordered bucket for tasks we might do. This bucket is another grass catcher. Furthermore, we have a monitor bucket for things we want to remember but that are the primary responsibility of others. Finally, we have an archive bucket, where we put important messages that don't have an associated action.

To mark a skimmed email unread is not emptying. Rather, it is doubling the energy cost you pay when you read and understand messages.[34] In total emptying, you move all messages to your personal system of prioritization, monitoring, and archiving.

SELECTIVE READING

Similar to email, high on the list of office irritation is the accumulation of books, magazines, web-based articles, and other texts we intend to read.[35] World speed reading champion Anne Jones read *Harry Potter and the Deathly Hallows* in 47 minutes.[36] However, ramping up our reading speed is a waste if we still don't get the main gist of what we're reading.

The practice of *speed reading* teaches us tips like how to move our eyes, cover up already read sentences, start every line on the second word, etc. It promises much, but unfortunately there's a trade-off between speed and accuracy. We must slow down to achieve good comprehension.[37]

James McCay rhetorically asked if you'd like to be able to read 50,000 words a minute: all you have to do is recognize within a minute that a 50,000-word text doesn't suit your purposes and decide not to read it.[38] Weeding out what to not read is the first step in *selective reading*.

Start by reading for the gist of the material. Read the table of contents carefully. Continue by reading the summaries of the three most interesting chapters. Then, choose one of these three and examine thought signposts like headings, bullet lists, diagrams, and other visual information.[39]

Finally, read the interesting paragraphs. Underline phrases that catch the major thoughts and make insight notes in the margin. Reiterate this process for other chapters until the value of reading more in this particular text is less than the value of reading something else.

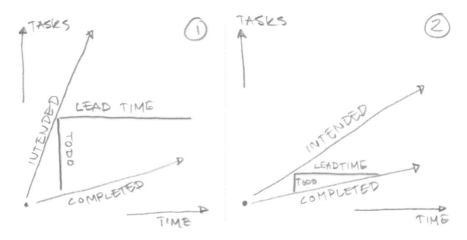

LIMIT YOUR TASK LIST

Little's Law says that the more tasks we plan to do, the longer it will take on average for a task to be completed. This is intuitive. If we're busy doing many things, then new tasks that unexpectedly become important must line up behind other tasks for a long time before we can handle them.

Lead time is the latency between the moment you write a new task on your to-do list and the moment you deliver the result. The number of tasks you put on your list is proportional to the lead time. The more tasks, the longer they'll stay on the to-do list.

This concept was presented by Alan Cobham in 1954[40] and proved by John Little in 1961.[41] You don't have to be a mathematician to realize that Little's Law is correct. The two charts above show the difference between having many tasks and having few tasks on your to-do list.

The most important task tomorrow might not even be a tiny idea today. Priorities change. The responsible attitude is to embrace change. We can only take on suddenly important tasks if we have flexible priorities. And flexibility in your priorities demands a limited number of tasks on your to-do list.

In the monotasking method, you have only two to-do lists: the *short list* and the *grass catcher list*. Remember: The short list is always limited to a maximum of five tasks. The grass catcher list is allowed to grow as ideas appear, but the practice of weekly weeding restores it to five tasks.

EFFECTIVE NO

Michael, a young client and ambitious knowledge worker, told me he was having a hard time. He wanted to impress his manager, but he was overwhelmed with so many requests that he couldn't complete things. It was easy to see that Michael had a problem with the word *"no."*

Saying *"yes"* when you mean *"no"* is bad for all parties involved; you just delay the discomfort of saying *"no."* And the person you gave the *"yes"* to builds her commitments on the false expectation that you will accomplish this task.

When someone asks you to take on a new task, ask yourself what you would have to give up in order to carry out this new request. Something must be removed from your agenda if you say *"yes."* Do a thought experiment and figure out what that thing would be.

If competing requests come from the same source, then you should involve that source in the prioritization process. In the case noted above, we agreed that Michael should tell his manager this: *"If you rank this new task higher than your other recent request, then I'd be happy to switch to it."*

A monotasker knows that only one task has top priority. A vague *"yes"* does not keep a line of retreat open. A *"yes"* is actually a *"yes."* Monotasking demands transparent as well as flexible priorities.

OPT-OUT CONDITIONS

Sometimes many other tasks become more important than the one you're working on. That's the number one reason for dropping a task from your list when that task hasn't been completed yet.

Another motive is that the expected return on investment isn't as good as you'd previously thought. Halfway through the task, you realize either that this task will take vastly more time than you thought or else that it won't deliver the value you had planned or expected. That's when you have to think about opting out.

Before you quit, here are three questions you should ask yourself:[42]

- **Am I panicking?** It's better to decide on a set of opt-out conditions in advance than to make an emotional move. For example: I'll give this project two days and see where it takes me.
- **Who am I trying to influence?** When your manager shows no interest in your result, quitting this task may seem plausible. Influencing a group is different. Before you quit, think twice about whether there are other stakeholders who are waiting on your results.
- **What sort of measurable progress am I making?** Sometimes opting out looks painful. But sticking with a task in the absence of forward progress is waste. Sometimes you need courage to stop it.

GRACEFUL OPT-OUT

However important a task is, it may not belong among our most important ones. Given that we discover new tasks every day, the less important tasks will never make it to our top priority spot. Unfortunately, stakeholders in that task will still believe they will get a result.

As painful as it may be, notifying stakeholders that you'll not perform a previously committed task is necessary. As long as the stakeholders think we're going to do their task, they will repeatedly disturb us by expressing a desire for progress reports.

The sooner you can inform others that you are renouncing your responsibility, the better for everyone. Never blame lack of time. Tell them instead that it's based on a prioritization of your tasks and that you want everyone to know about it, so that they can account for it in their future work.

You don't need to justify why this task isn't important or tell them what you've prioritized over their task. The relevant information for stakeholders is that you won't perform this task. Consider, however, whether you can suggest someone to take your place or an alternative solution for accomplishing the task.

Starting tasks without completing them costs energy and focus. *The waiter effect* taught us that.[43] Informing all stakeholders that you are opting out is a way to remove the task from your mind. Others will also respect you more when you are transparent with your priorities. It shows that you have integrity.

CALENDAR VS. TO-DO LIST

Which task should we pick next? In order to not waste brain energy, we don't want to assess every single potential option every time we need to move on to a new task. But neither do we want to rely on outdated priorities. Things may have happened that will impact our priorities.

Long to-do lists hide priorities. The green-green-red phenomenon[44] describes those times when everything seems fine for a long time and then suddenly it isn't. It's a chimera that we're on track, just because we have all the important tasks on our list. The status unexpectedly goes from green to red when we forget to start on them in time.

Can work catch our attention at the perfect time, if we schedule all tasks in our calendar? Unfortunately, no. New tasks arrive out of the blue. Some tasks take more time than we predicted. Even the slightest disturbance in our tight schedule can cause the whole system to crash.[45]

A flexible priority system makes it possible to easily adapt to unexpected changes in circumstances. Our priority system must also have a thorough and readable description of what we perceive as most important right now. We want neither outdated priorities nor adjustable chaos.

The monotasking method's *short list* is such a system. It's small, trimmed and kept up to date with no more than five of our most important tasks. We work—one at a time—on these *softscape* tasks, either during unscheduled time or during deliberately scheduled *discretionary time*.

DELEGATION

Delegation is never effortless. For sufficient results, you'll still need to be available to support the person to whom you delegated the task. You also introduce new risks, as you lose some control. However, if failure isn't critical, then delegation can be efficient as well as effective. Focus on achieving impact, not on requesting documents.

When you are selecting a colleague to help you with a task, there are a few important variables you should consider: Does the person have higher expertise than you in the task's area? Does the person currently have responsibility for less important tasks? Will delegation give the person a chance to grow? You must also check on whether she's authorized, committed, and reliable. Finally, accept the fact that the result won't be exactly the same as if you did the task yourself.

Make sure your colleague understands what you expect. Let her know that you sincerely believe in her ability to carry out this task. Explain the purpose of the task, not the method to solve it. She must have freedom of action in order to be committed.

Delegation doesn't reduce your responsibility. It's critical to schedule a synchronization meeting in the near future. Define a minimal progress to be made before that appointment. Seeing is believing—seeing tangible progress after 10–25 percent of the total expected time needed to complete the task will give you an idea of her speed and direction.

If your colleague shows no concrete results at your first synchronization meeting, ask her if she's committed. Perceived lack of time or inability to get in touch with the right people are triggers to stop throwing good money after bad ideas. Consider voiding this delegation promptly.

VITAL FEW, USEFUL MANY

In 1937, Joseph Juran conceptualized the 80/20 rule, sometimes called the *Pareto principle*.[46] It says that a minority of causes creates the majority of effects. While 80 percent of our tasks are useful, or perhaps even trivial, only 20 percent of the tasks are vital. The few vital tasks create almost all the value.

The story goes that Warren Buffet initially told Mike Flint to make a list of his top twenty-five career goals. Then Warren instructed Mike to circle the top five. Finally Warren gave some surprising advice about the bottom twenty: *"No matter what, these things get no attention from you until you've succeeded with your top five."*[47] Note that deliberately avoiding a task is not the same as deferring it.

Can we choose to do all the tasks that create value? No. If we complete the top five tasks and save twenty, then tomorrow we'll probably have at least five new tasks. These five new tasks will most likely be more important than the twenty we saved from the day before. So, why keep these tasks, which we obviously won't do?

The waiter effect teaches us that tasks we don't finish will demand our attention.[48] They will make us less focused on our few vital tasks, those top five. In the worst case, we'll even put effort into tasks that clearly have little or no impact, just to satisfy stakeholders or get some peace of mind. Started but never finished tasks are wasted time.

Weeding is the method of finally dropping tasks we know deep down that we'll never complete. Once a week, we copy our five most important tasks from the old *grass catcher list* to a fresh one. Then we inform all stakeholders that we won't do the rest because their priority is too low.

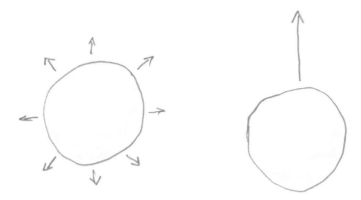

ESSENTIALISM

Could it be that we perform better if we become more selective? Instead of being eager to jump onto every bandwagon, we can choose to focus on what really matters.

Greg McKeown teaches us, in his book *Essentialism*[49], we must understand three realities before we can recognize what is most essential:

- **Individual choice:** We can choose where we want to place our attention and how we want to spend our time. It is not easy to say no, but we must understand that we have the power to do so.
- **Existence of noise:** Almost everything is noise, but a few things are extremely valuable. Only if we make the effort to find the most important things can we be in the position to avoid the noise.
- **Tradeoffs:** We can't do everything. A tradeoff means opting out of things that are not top priority, even if they seem fun.

Essentialism is not just about getting more done by doing fewer things. It is as much about quality as quantity. By focusing on the most important thing, we can achieve the best possible result, doing less but doing it better.

This is vital in the monotasking method. There are so many interesting and potentially fun projects out there. We can't spend our time on all of them. Knowing what's essential and sticking to that is the way to go.

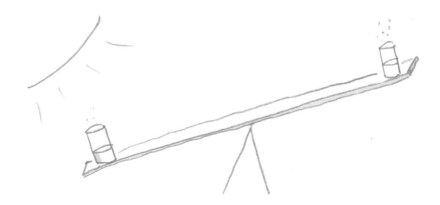

THE THREE LAWS OF PRIORITY DYNAMICS

The laws of priority dynamics describe how quantities like priority and productivity behave under various circumstances (much like the laws of thermodynamics).[50]

0. Every task request you responded to with an unreserved *"yes"* has the same priority. Saying *"yes"* to many things implies that you believe they can be done in a random order. A prioritized to-do list is not a yes-list; rather, it's a list ordered by task importance.

1. Priority can neither be created nor destroyed. It can only be transferred from one task to another. When you raise the priority of one task, you automatically lower the priority of all other tasks.

2. The value of a previously prioritized to-do list always decreases as time progresses. If you don't reprioritize regularly based on your recent knowledge, then your plan is doomed to be dysfunctional.

3. Trying to do everything at the same time gives the same result as doing nothing: you don't complete anything. Monotasking maximizes your productivity.

CUT DOWN ON TASKS TO DO – SUMMARY

Q: What are the key benefits of using the short list?
A: With no more than five tasks, the most important ones right now, we can disconnect from tasks we can't or shouldn't do right now. The small number of tasks also makes it possible to use our intuition in prioritizing them. When in *panorama mode*, put an "x" next to the most important task on your short list and focus on that one solely during the next monotasking session.

Q: What are the grass catcher list and weeding?
A: Tasks and ideas that don't make it to the limited short list right now can be saved in the *grass catcher list*. This list is not ordered or limited. Once a week, however, you replace it with a new grass catcher list. This process is called *weeding*. Copy the most important tasks—but not more than five—from the old grass catcher list to a new grass catcher list. Then run your old grass catcher list through the shredder.

Q: I understand the 80/20 rule: While many tasks are useful, only a few are vital. The latter are responsible for the majority of the impact I make. However, is there something wrong with keeping the useful many in my to-do list?
A: Yes, there is. You will probably never complete the useful many. By the time you've completed the vital few, new vital tasks will have appeared (and by the way, there's no limit to how many valuable tasks we humans can imagine). The useful many tasks are then just noise, competing for your attention—for no reason. The *waiter effect* teaches us that reducing our to-do list protects our mind from irrelevant thoughts.[51]

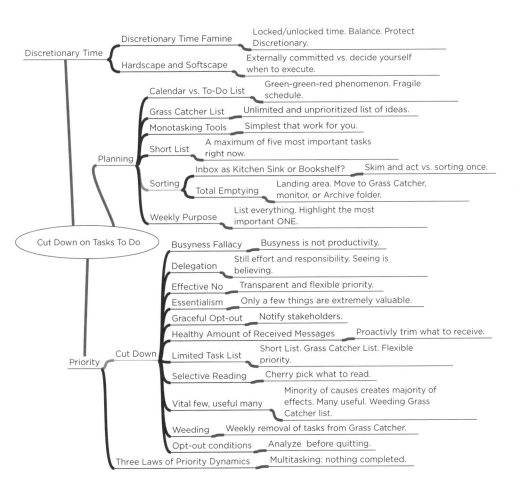

Cut Down on Tasks To Do

Discretionary Time
- Discretionary Time Famine — Locked/unlocked time. Balance. Protect Discretionary.
- Hardscape and Softscape — Externally committed vs. decide yourself when to execute.

Planning
- Calendar vs. To-Do List — Green-green-red phenomenon. Fragile schedule.
- Grass Catcher List — Unlimited and unprioritized list of ideas.
- Monotasking Tools — Simplest that work for you.
- Short List — A maximum of five most important tasks right now.
- Sorting
  - Inbox as Kitchen Sink or Bookshelf? — Skim and act vs. sorting once.
  - Total Emptying — Landing area. Move to Grass Catcher, monitor, or Archive folder.
- Weekly Purpose — List everything. Highlight the most important ONE.

Priority

Cut Down
- Busyness Fallacy — Busyness is not productivity.
- Delegation — Still effort and responsibility. Seeing is believing.
- Effective No — Transparent and flexible priority.
- Essentialism — Only a few things are extremely valuable.
- Graceful Opt-out — Notify stakeholders.
- Healthy Amount of Received Messages — Proactivly trim what to receive.
- Limited Task List — Short List. Grass Catcher List. Flexible priority.
- Selective Reading — Cherry pick what to read.
- Vital few, useful many — Minority of causes creates majority of effects. Many useful. Weeding Grass Catcher list.
- Weeding — Weekly removal of tasks from Grass Catcher.
- Opt-out conditions — Analyze before quitting.

Three Laws of Priority Dynamics — Multitasking: nothing completed.

CHAPTER 3
FOCUS ON ONE TASK NOW

ONCE WE'VE PRIORITIZED AND initiated a task, there is nothing positive in trying to focus on several things at once. It's just as true when you chose the second interrupting task yourself as when you are interrupted by other people. Task switching has devastating effects on our performance.

We must take back our day. Both the office environment and our thoughts need to be cleared of alternate tasks and other disturbing elements. The focus should be on focusing. We also need a method to effectively manage other people's desire for help without reducing the pace of our own work.

This chapter presents hands-on methods like *notification celibacy* and *volunteer hour* to help you stay focused on one task at a time. It also shows how fatal the consequences of constant task switching are. Rather than juggling many tasks at the same time, you should aim to ignore all tasks except the most important one.

IN ONE MINUTE: HOW TO FOCUS ON ONE TASK NOW

Five simple concepts:

- **Human multitasking is a myth** that makes employers search for people who can juggle many tasks at once. When we think we're multitasking, we're actually task switching. Task switching induces more errors in what we do and slows us down.
- **Monotasking and panorama sessions** create a rhythm for you. Monotasking means zooming in on one and only one task. Panorama means seeing the bigger picture and choosing the most important task for right now. You switch between the two.
- **Notification celibacy** is the practice of having audio and visual alerts on your electronic devices disabled when you monotask. It takes more than a minute to recover to the same speed after seeing an email notification.[52] Automatic notifications let the *waiter effect* work against our valuable task focus.[53]
- **Volunteer hour** is a concrete strategy for interruption recovery. You steer your colleagues' wish for conversation to a scheduled meeting in the afternoon. It gives you breathing space for work and it gives your colleague a more prepared interlocutor.
- **Time pressure** is shaped within ourselves. People may claim that their task is urgent, but time pressure is our own construction. The monotasking method makes us confident that we do our best when we prioritize important tasks over urgent tasks.

Questionnaire:

In order to kickstart your neurons, put a checkmark next to every statement below that you consider to be a recurring time robber in your current workplace.

- ☐ Task switching
- ☐ Casual visitors
- ☐ Regular meetings
- ☐ Ambiguous checklists
- ☐ Smart phone notifications
- ☐ Too few breaks
- ☐ Spontaneous phone calls
- ☐ Everyday administration
- ☐ Too many people involved in trivial decision making
- ☐ Misplaced information
- ☐ Canceled meetings

- ☐ No stakeholders present
- ☐ Business trips
- ☐ Poor video conference facilities
- ☐ Conflicting directives
- ☐ Changed decisions without anchoring
- ☐ Desire for perfection
- ☐ High responsibility and low authority
- ☐ Ignorant subcontractors
- ☐ Involving everyone

A CUCUMBER AND AN ARTICHOKE MEET AT THE CIRCUS

Cucumber: How was your day?

Artichoke: Good. I'm happy I can juggle so many balls. My manager is impressed.

Cucumber: Did you complete anything?

Artichoke: No, unfortunately not. Juggling keeps me busy, but the drawback is that I'm merely running from meeting to meeting instead of actually producing anything.

Cucumber: Do you know why the zebra has stripes?

Artichoke: No, but I guess it's for protection in some way.

Cucumber: The zebra stripes confuse the lion. Each individual's stripes blend in with the stripes of the other members of the herd around this particular zebra. The lion has trouble picking out any one zebra and so she can't make a plan for how to attack. She can't even understand in which direction the zebra is moving. The predator doesn't see the prey; it can only see a lot of stripes—hundreds or thousands—moving around in an unpredictable pattern.

Artichoke: Okay?

Cucumber: Think of each zebra as a task on your to-do list. You are the lion that needs to focus on one zebra at a time. Your work-in-progress mustn't be the number of individuals in the zebra herd. Your effort to complete any task depends on your success in separating a zebra from the herd. Furthermore, to complete the most important task—to be maximally effective—you must separate the *right* zebra from the herd.

Artichoke: You mean, I should juggle a single ball and ignore the rest?

Cucumber: Exactly.

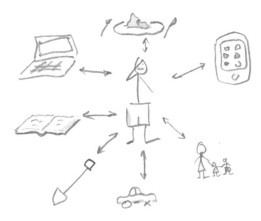

THE MYTH OF MULTITASKING

Ability to multitask used to be put in job descriptions as a requirement. Juggling many tasks improves efficiency, doesn't it? Actually, no. Human multitasking is a myth, a fallacy. It doesn't exist. In the future, monotasking may well be the most sought-after capability. It should be.

Research shows that we can't multitask. The brain isn't able to pay attention to more than one thing at a time.[54] When we believe we're multitasking, we're constantly task switching. It gives us an illusion of control. In addition, it might make us look very efficient to others. But we're not.

Task switching induces more errors in what we do, and it slows us down.[55] Our performance declines. Doing one thing, interrupting ourselves, doing another thing, and then jumping back again to the first thing—it's devastating for productivity. Each task switch costs time and costs brain energy.

Nobel Prize laureate Herbert Simon wrote that humans operate largely in serial fashion. In addition, he said that the more demanding a task is, the more single-minded we are.[56] To maximize productivity, we must pick the most important task and inhibit all other tasks.

Peter Drucker revealed that the one secret of effectiveness is concentration. Do first things first and do one thing at a time.[57] In the monotasking method, we choose one task while we're in panorama mode. We then focus exclusively on that task for a limited time in monotask mode.

WORKING MEMORY CAPACITY

In 1956, George A. Miller argued that the number of objects an average person can hold in working memory is about seven.[58] An object can be a chunk of data. For example, it is not hard to remember the sequence 0123456789, even though it's ten numbers.

In 2001, Nelson Cowan revised this magic number to three simultaneous chunks in an accessible state.[59] Brian McElree showed the same year that we can only maintain one unit in our focal attention.[60] Attention is about processing and working memory is about accessible state.

If we think of our working memory as a very limited scratchpad, it becomes obvious why monotasking is inevitable in order to achieve results. Everything on the scratchpad is wiped off when your problem solving is interrupted by a competing task.

Checking your inbox every now and then is an effective way to destroy your productivity.[61] It's also crucial to dissociate the *monotasking session* from the *panorama session*. Prioritizing tasks requires a lot of brain energy and can't be done while you are working on a task.

Thinking with a pencil in your hand[62] is a great trick to compensate for the limits of working memory. Mind maps, however simple, help you maintain multiple thoughts simultaneously. They also let you quickly recover your thoughts rather than lose them when you're distracted by someone.

ATTENTION TYPES

We are exposed to a constant flow of audio, visual, and other stimuli. The brain processes what comes in but can't keep up with everything. Attention is the brain function that concentrates our processing capacity on one task. It can be controlled by both our will and noisy stimuli.

Here's a model of five different kinds of attention in order of difficulty:[63]

1. **Focused attention:** You have the ability to notice sounds or other events in your surroundings.
2. **Sustained attention:** You focus on one and only one task, such as writing an email to a client.
3. **Selective attention:** You manage to maintain focus on a task, despite your own irrelevant thoughts or things happening around you.
4. **Alternating Attention:** You switch rapidly between two related tasks like listening to a lecture and taking notes on interesting things.
5. **Divided attention:** You do two things at once, called multitasking. To be successful, all but one task must be automated, like walking. If we really try to focus on two unrelated things, we actually alternate between tasks.[64]

Monotasking is all about the third type of attention. The easiest way to complete more is to maintain focus for a while on one single task—that is, using your selective attention.

10 - 12 - 7 - 19 - 14 - 8 - 17

COST OF TASK SWITCHING

Arthur Jersild did an interesting study way back in 1927. This was before smart phones, computers, and television. He recruited participants and divided them into two groups. In the first group, participants worked through a list of numbers like the one above. They were instructed to subtract three from each number. The time it took to write down the sums was measured.

The other group got to go through the same list, but this group performed more than one task. They added six to every second number and subtracted three from the rest. Of course, it took a significantly longer time. The obvious reason is that they switched tasks.[65]

The fact that task switchers pay a price has been tested and validated many times since. Research has found that we lose more time when we switch to more complex tasks. The cost also increases when we switch to unfamiliar tasks.[66]

It's hard to put an exact number on the task-switching price tag. However, the undisputable knowledge that it's a significant amount is enough for us to understand that decreasing task switching will make us more productive.

And it's not only about losing time. Because we must empty our working memory when we switch tasks, we'll easily forget what we were doing. An intuitive idea about how we could solve this task might not come back. In the worst case, we don't even remember what task we were focused on.

MALICIOUS FEEDBACK LOOP

So human multitasking is a myth. We can't pay full attention to two things simultaneously. We might think we can, but we're actually switching rapidly between tasks. And this switching has a cognitive cost.

As soon as our brain resources are divided among tasks, our effectiveness goes down. For instance, behavioral studies have shown that engaging in a secondary task, such as talking on a mobile phone, disrupts driving performance.[67]

Unfortunately, our brain encourages us to switch tasks. Every time we manage to complete a small task, like answering an email or checking an update on social media, the brain sends out a little shot of the reward hormone dopamine. The little achievement makes us feel proud and satisfied.

Thus, interrupting ourselves to do small, meaningless things is a bad habit created by the malicious feedback loop of dopamine rewards. We think we've done something productive when the truth is that we spoiled our focus on the most important task.

The monotasking method is designed to fight this habit. Pick one task. Be fully aware of what task it is. Set the alarm to the next vertical position of the clock's minute hand, at least twenty-five minutes away. Focus on this task as if nothing else matters until the alarm rings.

NOTIFICATION CELIBACY

We have chosen Task A. It's the most important one. But our smartphone and computer flash and beep while we try to focus on A. It's not multitasking. In our eagerness to be busy and recognized, and to not miss anything, we allow ourselves to be continuously disturbed by digital notifications.

A case study by the Danwood Group found that, on average, it takes more than a minute to recover to the same speed after seeing an email notification. Moreover, the majority of all emails were viewed within six seconds of receiving the notification.[68] That's even quicker than letting the phone ring three times.

Quite simply, the anticipation of a new message is self-rewarded by our brain. Application manufacturers know that. The *waiter effect* will force us to think about the message we just saw.[69] We want to be productive, but the app would prefer us to spend all our time with it.

Continuously giving a task only part of our attention[70] is not a productive behavior. We switch between input streams of messages. Task A is important, but the notifications are perceived as urgent. The brain believes that we're doing something when we respond to a new notification. Actually, we're producing nothing.

In order to achieve results with Task A, you must replace push with pull. You get to decide when you want to check your inbox. In *notification celibacy*, you eliminate all automatic notifications from your phone and computer. Now less willpower is needed in order to focus on Task A.

CONCENTRATION MODEL

Christina Bengtsson spent twenty-five thousand hours on the shooting range before becoming a world champion in military precision shooting. To get the gold medal, she developed a method called *the concentration model*.[71] The model consists of three steps.

You're trying to focus on a task, but your thoughts wander. The first step is to notice what you are thinking about. What will I cook for dinner tonight? Is my neighbor angry with me? What time will I pick up my son from school? These thoughts distract you.

The second step is to place the distracting thought on an imagined timeline. The two centered vertical bars represent the *Now*. To the left is the *Past*. To the right is the *Future*. For example, *"What time will I pick up Mia?"* goes to the right horizontal line.

Finally, you replace these thoughts from the *Past* or the *Future* with a neutral thought that is in the very *Now*. You can, for example, think for a moment about the spelling or the font in the document you're writing. Or you may think about how you place your fingers on the keyboard.

Christina defines concentration as freedom from distracting thoughts about the future and the past, freedom from demands and anxiety. No doubts. No ifs or whys. Humans have this great ability to imagine the future and analyze the past. Sometimes we need to temporarily turn it off.

PROSPECTIVE MEMORY

A week ago, you decided to call your mother on her birthday. Still, you failed to remember it yesterday, on her actual birthday. *Prospective memory* is when we intend to do something at a later time. It's as much about memory as planning and task management.[72]

In a significant number of all airline accidents, the highly motivated expert pilots have forgotten to follow their ordinary procedures. Distractions, absence of cues that normally prompt performance of habitual tasks, habit capture, and multitasking are the reasons.[73]

Hardscapes are tasks that are bound to be executed at a certain time; for example, meetings. Use external memory aids, like calendar alerts on your smartphone (but don't check for them when you're in a monotasking session), to help you remember these. *Softscapes* must be on the *short list* or the *grass catcher list*.

Avoid multitasking when you do a critical multi-step task. Even if we remember to do this task, we might miss one step in the performance procedure. The failure happens when we become engaged with other tasks and lose attention on the task we originally intended to do.

If a very important task suddenly shows up, then do it the very next monotasking session instead of deferring it further. If you're not in the place to do it now, then create a reminder cue and place it where it's likely to be encountered. Relying on prospective memory can be dangerous.

ATTENTIONAL BLINK BOTTLENECK

You listen to your boss's review of the upcoming week's challenges. Simultaneously, you observe that the colleague next to you is taking notes with a fancy pen. Suddenly, your boss asks you: *"Can you help us with this task?"* What task? You didn't catch what he said at all.

Our brain's ability to process new events is like our eyesight when we blink. While the eye is closed, we risk missing something. The brain is sometimes closed as well. While we process the first event, we're unable to catch new events. It's called *attentional blink bottleneck*.[74]

In an experiment exploring this phenomenon, participants saw a stream of letters and numbers; ten new characters every second. All the characters were black except one white. Participants were told to identify the latter. They were also instructed to tell if they saw a black X right after the white character.[75]

When the X was shown shortly after the white character, it was almost impossible for the participants to observe it. Since their brains were in the middle of processing the white character, they couldn't receive more information. The attentional bottleneck prevented them from noticing the X.

We can't perform a task well if we are simultaneously having a chit-chat with our cubicle neighbor, getting beeps and visual alerts on our smartphones, or if we're looking around to see who went to lunch. The attentional bottleneck blocks awareness and disrupts decision-making.

CASUAL VISITORS

Lily is a manager and she complained to me about drop-in visitors who interrupt her discretionary time. They didn't make an effort to arrange an appointment. She wanted to be polite, but she had learned that *"I don't have time"* is a no-no phrase. What could she do?

The first thing is always to stand up immediately when someone enters your working space. It'll decrease the conversation time. The second thing is to really understand their number one desire. Are they looking for chit-chatting? Do they need some information you have? If so, what information?

If you've focused hard on some task for more than an hour, then this might be a welcome and energizing break. Otherwise, only deal with their request now if it's truly brief or a genuine emergency. Still, you can make progress by making an appointment or redirecting them.

Direct them to the right person if you don't have the information they need. Don't have long and speculative rambles about what the solution might be, since neither of you knows that. But, if you really are the one who can help them, schedule a meeting so that you can be prepared.

Non-work-related visits also warrant a win-win solution. Schedule a lunch[76] where you've got enough time for gossiping or chatting about the latest celebrity news. Then you can also spend a moment looking at vacation photos or hear your colleague's report on newborn family members.

VOLUNTEER HOUR

My client Saša was convinced that she couldn't possibly work in time boxes. She was always interrupted by subordinates.[77] Her observation was that it's a duty in her role as manager to be at the heart of things, to always be prepared to help others. In the latter, she was right.

She tried blocking out an hour after lunch every day in her calendar. We called it *the volunteer hour*. When colleagues requested her helping hand during the day, she—instantly without dissecting the problem—scheduled a 15-to-30-minute meeting in her next volunteer hour.

This concrete and simple action plan made her interruption recovery smooth and quick. No momentum was lost for the work she monotasked on right before she was distracted. On days where no request for help appeared, she spent her volunteer hour on discretionary work.

Naturally, there are exceptions. When Saša could answer a question from the top of her head, she did so immediately. Sudden high-risk tasks also had a higher priority than her volunteer hour strategy. But, how often can a task not be deferred a few hours?

Already after a few weeks, Saša told me how successful the *volunteer hour* strategy is. She used it also for incoming phone calls that required more thoughts and discussions. An added bonus was the fact that the *waiter effect*[78] let her subconsciously process the task ahead.

FACILITATING MUSIC

Music can influence the efficiency of simple repetitive tasks in a positive way.[79] However, modern office work is seldom repetitive. If we want to understand the impact of listening to music, we must consider parameters like music preference, volume, and peacefulness.

When choosing to listen to music while doing cognitively challenging tasks, we sometimes intend to mask the focus-killing presence of intelligible speech[80]—especially one-sided overheard phone conversations, which are terribly distracting.[81] Another reason to listen to music is to bolster our creativity.

Intelligible speech has been proven to be distracting, so it seems reasonable that music without lyrics is a better choice than music with lyrics. Fewer cognitive resources are available when your attention is drawn to the lyrics. Studies have even shown that we perform worse while listening to our preferred type of music.[82]

Listening to sedative music gives better performance results than listening to stimulative music.[83] So maybe we should go for nature sounds at moderate volume. One study showed that workers enhanced their ability to concentrate when they were exposed to the sound of flowing water in a mountain stream.[84]

Silence is probably the most productive environment for cognitive activity.[85] This is, however, usually not an option in modern, open-plan offices. If you choose to listen to music, you might want to pick familiar music without lyrics or a strong emotional component.

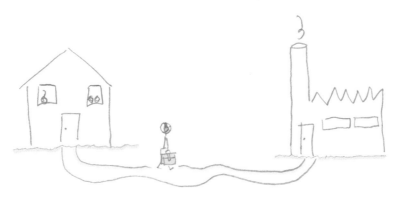

TRANSITION TIME

Kai spends three hours a day commuting. Her manager promises she'll get paid if she works while traveling. Commuting is one type of what's more generally called *transition time*—transition in between work and private thinking mode. Kai and I came up with a strategy for this.

Office work consists mostly of writing, reading, and verbal communication. Verbal communication and writing are not comfortable when commuting, but reading is. Always keep a nonfiction book in your briefcase and make sure you save any minutes for upcoming meetings to read during your commute.[86]

Transition time also includes the very last minutes before you leave the office. If spent well, they can have a vast impact. Put a note on your desk, stating what you'll start with tomorrow morning. The *waiter effect* will start your subconscious problem-solving process for this task.[87]

Transition time can even be the time from waking up until we leave home. For most people, 5 a.m. is a time when life is calm and distractions are completely absent. Some people use this time of the day for making their daily plan and blocking discretionary time in their schedule.[88]

Kai also started to have productive coffee breaks and lunches, and she listened to podcasts while driving. All these habits made a striking difference for her. Her manager was impressed enough to promote her to an executive position!

CHECKLISTS

Checklists have proven to be very useful in order to avoid aviation safety incidents. The fallibility of human memory and attention jeopardizes routine tasks as well as emergency situations. Another example is a surgical safety checklist that declined the rate of death by almost 50 percent.[89]

There are two types of checklists: Do-Confirm and Read-Do.[90] In Do-Confirm we merely check that everything is OK. Did we receive payments for all sent invoices? Read-Do is handy when we have a manual procedure. How do I turn off the office alarm system in the morning?

Checklists are particularly handy in repetitive projects that we perform too infrequently for them to be second nature, for example taxes or setting up some system on the computer. Every time you make stupid mistakes that cause failure, create a new checklist for that procedure.

Keep the checklist simple: between five and nine steps in precise but not verbose wording. It's tempting to shortcut the instructions if they are complicated, thinking that this has never happened before and thus will never happen again. Pinpoint mandatory and hard to recall identities, like server names and phone numbers.

Continually refine your checklists. Every time you execute the list and either misunderstand something or miss a critical identity, it's time to update it. Also, when there are too many steps or it takes more than ten minutes to follow the checklist, break it down into all-or-none procedures.

CORNELL NOTES

An action point was assigned to you at a business meeting. You work hard to meet the requirements, but at the follow-up meeting people are disappointed with you. They say you solved the wrong problem. Did you really recall what the action point was?

Cornell notes is a technique that's been around since the 1950s, first explained by Walter Pauk.[91] To take Cornell notes, you split the paper vertically. The column on the left is for post-meeting questions, main ideas, and diagrams. Live writing during meeting is to the right. The summary is at the bottom.

Note-taking is not only for recording things exactly. It's also about learning and synthesizing. A tool that demands a slower pace has been proven to be effective. The more you analyze and write in your own words, instead of rephrasing verbatim, the more you'll remember.[92]

That's why studies have shown that writing with a pen on paper is more effective than taking notes on a laptop.[93] Because keyboard writing is more efficient than longhand, we're tempted to just literally transcribe what people say without thinking about what we are writing.

In the Cornell notes technique, you write in the upper right section during the meeting. Within twenty-four hours, you add pulled-out questions to the left and add a summary at the bottom. Right before the follow-up meeting, you cover the right part and attempt to answer the questions.

PREOCCUPATION

Half the meeting done and the moderator asks you a question. *"Huhh?"* Not that you were sleeping, but your thoughts had wandered. How can I write the project report? Who was I going to call tomorrow? You were thinking about everything but the meeting you were supposed to be participating in.

When you're preoccupied, you don't manage your time. Rather, you're wasting it. The antidote to preoccupation is relevance.[94] Here are some things that might help you win back your meeting attention:

- **Cultivate observation:** In your particular expert area, you see things other people don't see. Look around. One colleague looks busy but never delivers. Another one wrote an excellent report. Your manager is great at presenting bad news.
- **Think with a pencil in your hand:** Write your ideas down while you're thinking. Visualize outstanding questions where the meeting isn't unanimous.
- **Make comparisons:** Compare what your colleagues don't know with something you're mutually familiar with. Make your point with a metaphor from your shared domain.
- **Use a spontaneous goal:** As you're entering a meeting, ask yourself, *"What's the purpose of this meeting?"*

Participating in a meeting while being preoccupied is one of the most unproductive ways of spending your time—and the time of others. Set the standard to always find relevance.

TIME PRESSURE

My client Javier told me that he was both more productive and more creative when facing an imminent deadline. He claimed that a deadline was mandatory to get him going. However, he didn't like the stress it created.

Time pressure is shaped within ourselves. People may strongly demand that we immediately spend our time on their tasks. Their demands give us excuses for creating time pressure, but the time pressure is built by ourselves. With monotasking, we don't need time pressure.

A study conducted by Harvard Business School[95] found that high time pressure has a negative impact on creative thinking. Curiously, even though the experiment gave evidence of *less* creative thinking under time pressure, the participants' own feeling was that they were more creative.

Perceived time pressure also appears to be negative for decision making. That's why we perform worse in decision-making games like the *Iowa Gambling Task* when we're told that there's not sufficient time to learn and complete the game.[96]

We solved Javier's problems by agreeing that time will come to us at a constant speed. There's no doubt about that. By monotasking his most important task, he used his time in the best way possible. There is no other way to complete things more quickly or achieve better results.

FOCUS ON ONE TASK NOW – SUMMARY

Q: Doing two things in parallel doubles my speed, doesn't it? Or is there a cost associated with task switching and multitasking?

A: Human multitasking is only possible for tasks that do not require attention, like breathing or walking. We might think we're multitasking, but we're actually *task switching.* The latter comes with a heavy price: Numerous studies show that task switching slows us down, causes us to make more mistakes, and harms our creativity.

Q: Monotasking sounds fine. But as an important project leader, I'm at the heart of things. Should I stop cooperating with others?

A: No, you should continue to cooperate with others to maximize your joint impact. However, by using the *volunteer hour* strategy, you can manage casual visitors more effectively without decreasing your contribution to others. The bonus is that you'll complete more of your discretionary work.

Q: Focusing unconditionally on one task makes me efficient, but how can I make sure that it's the right task? Priorities change all the time and I want to do what's most important right now.

A: Focusing on one task—without questioning whether it's the most important one—is mandatory for efficiency. But to be effective, we must reassess our priorities regularly. The monotasking/panorama rhythm starts with setting the *panorama cue* alarm to the next half or full hour. Then you look over the panorama of potential tasks to do next. Pick the most important one and focus on that one unconditionally until the next panorama cue. *Notification celibacy* (turning off automatic email downloads and every visual and audio app notification) will dramatically improve your focus success.

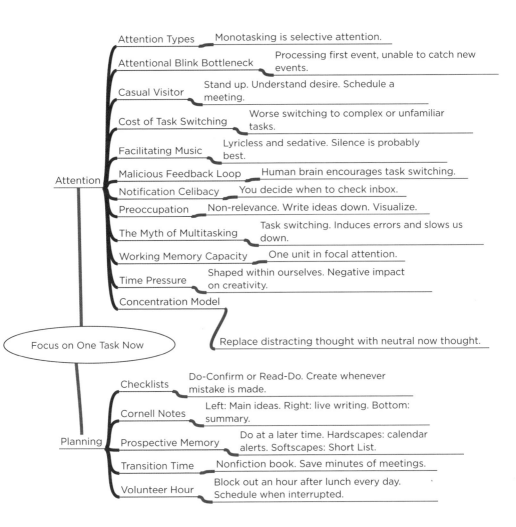

Focus on One Task Now

Attention

- Attention Types — Monotasking is selective attention.
- Attentional Blink Bottleneck — Processing first event, unable to catch new events.
- Casual Visitor — Stand up. Understand desire. Schedule a meeting.
- Cost of Task Switching — Worse switching to complex or unfamiliar tasks.
- Facilitating Music — Lyricless and sedative. Silence is probably best.
- Malicious Feedback Loop — Human brain encourages task switching.
- Notification Celibacy — You decide when to check inbox.
- Preoccupation — Non-relevance. Write ideas down. Visualize.
- The Myth of Multitasking — Task switching. Induces errors and slows us down.
- Working Memory Capacity — One unit in focal attention.
- Time Pressure — Shaped within ourselves. Negative impact on creativity.
- Concentration Model — Replace distracting thought with neutral now thought.

Planning

- Checklists — Do-Confirm or Read-Do. Create whenever mistake is made.
- Cornell Notes — Left: Main ideas. Right: live writing. Bottom: summary.
- Prospective Memory — Do at a later time. Hardscapes: calendar alerts. Softscapes: Short List.
- Transition Time — Nonfiction book. Save minutes of meetings.
- Volunteer Hour — Block out an hour after lunch every day. Schedule when interrupted.

CHAPTER 4
NEVER PROCRASTINATE

ISN'T IT PURE WASTE when we have decided what to do but we still don't do it? Especially since we often escape into meaningless trivia. In some way or another, our minds are not prepared to do the thing we want to do. Procrastination puts us in a troublesome position.

The first step in overcoming this problem is understanding the nature of our procrastination. There are many potential reasons. And with a little help from the *waiter effect*,[97] we can turn things around. We can make our brains eager to do instead of reluctant to do.

This chapter presents hands-on methods like *auto-insisting tasks* and *brain economy*. Avoiding procrastination is mostly about getting started. If we put a lot of effort into protecting our *discretionary time*, then we must not waste it on something other than the chosen task.

IN ONE MINUTE: HOW TO NEVER PROCRASTINATE

Five simple concepts:

- **Time inconsistency** is the belief that we'll be busier in the immediate future, and then less busy later on. Researchers have documented this human misconception. The treatment is to do the most important task right now. Urgency is not a valid argument.

- **Discretionary time waste** is when you have cordoned off time to work on your most important task, but you still do something else. We must make sure that we place a high value on our discretionary time. We can never get back wasted time.

- **The waiter effect** teaches us that we tend to better remember unfinished tasks.[98] If this principle is used correctly, it can help us to stop procrastinating. Used incorrectly, it will increase our procrastination. Subconscious thinking can promote the most important tasks over other tasks.

- **Self-fulfilling tasks** are an extension of the waiter effect. Maria Ovsiankina showed that humans have a strong will to complete interrupted tasks.[99] Starting a task before leaving the office in the afternoon will encourage you to continue with it when you return in the morning.

- **Intrinsic motivation** is superior to rewards and punishments. Autonomy is when you take responsibility for your own choices. Mastery is the mindset when you always want to improve. A motivating purpose is something bigger than yourself.

Questionnaire:

In order to kickstart your neurons, put a checkmark next to every statement below that you consider to be a recurring time robber in your current workplace.

☐ Deferred decisions
☐ Noisy colleagues
☐ Working Saturdays
☐ Non-challenging tasks
☐ Routine tasks
☐ Estimates interpreted as promises
☐ Hard to find information
☐ High responsibility and low authority
☐ Vague goals
☐ Low morale

☐ Pet projects
☐ Fear of opposing management
☐ Lack of IT competence
☐ Conflicting directives
☐ Fear of taking risks
☐ Uninspiring mornings
☐ Emerging deadlines
☐ Lack of privacy
☐ Constant distractions
☐ Three-hour meetings without breaks

A CUCUMBER AND AN ARTICHOKE MEET AT THE YACHT CLUB

Cucumber: How was your day at work?

Artichoke: Good. I had a delicious pesto pasta for lunch and during the afternoon coffee break, my colleague Josh told me the most fantastic story about how he started doing martial arts.

Cucumber: Did you complete any of your tasks?

Artichoke: No, unfortunately not. I'm responsible for an extremely boring project. The mission is so big, I don't know where to start. And the customer is the grumpy type who will probably complain, no matter what I deliver. I didn't want to be a member of this project in the first place. My boss forced me.

Cucumber: So, instead of getting started, you had a long lunch and then a long coffee break?

Artichoke: Is there something wrong with lunches and coffee breaks?

Cucumber: Absolutely not! They are perfect opportunities to recharge the brain and come up with new creative ideas. Your problem seems to be how you spent the rest of your time.

Artichoke: True. I know what to do, but I'm not doing it. I'm a procrastinator.

Cucumber: You don't have to be if you accept the pros and cons of your project and try making the best of it.

Artichoke: You know, Josh said today that one of the codes of his martial art order was *"I can't prevent the wind from blowing, but I can adjust my sails to make it work for me."*

Cucumber: How true. That's exactly my point.

Artichoke: Tomorrow, I'll break down my project into small increments and focus on a minimum viable idea. I already have something in mind.

TIME INCONSISTENCY

You seemed to have plenty of time when you said *"yes"* to the important task of investigating how to improve corporate cost control. Now—a month later, and with one day left before the board meeting where you're supposed to present your findings—you haven't even started.

Time inconsistency is when we think that we are unusually busy in the immediate future but will become less busy soon. Research shows that people expect slack time to be greater in the future than in the present.[100] Distant deadlines feel easy to meet.[101]

Remember how Eisenhower said that urgent tasks are not important, and the important ones are never urgent?[102] If we prioritize with respect to urgency, we'll often forget the important tasks. Students who do their homework the first day instead of the last evening usually get good results on the test.

You may think that it is about saying *"no"* more often, but it's not that simple. Many tasks may seem important when we get the request. Instead of the false dichotomy of yes/no, we must share our priorities with this task's stakeholders. Is it reasonable that we will carry it out in light of our other priorities?

Do capture everything. But work continuously on your priorities. Frequent and ruthless weeding makes it easier to predict your future performance. Also, break down larger tasks. Regular deliveries of viable interim results show whether you will be able to complete the whole task.

FLOW AND PROCRASTINATION

Procrastination is when we're fully aware that we should be doing Task A, but we escape to Task B and leave Task A untouched. *Flow* is when we're fully absorbed in the task we're focusing on.[103] Sounds like bad guy and good guy? Almost, but not completely.

We procrastinate for many reasons: Someone else wants me to do this; what's in it for me? This task is too big; where should I start? I'm afraid the result won't be good enough, so I don't want to deliver. I'm exhausted and need a break. I'm distracted by multiple tasks.

Procrastination should not be confused with TTT—thoughts take time.[104] Faced with a tricky problem, you may find a better solution if you digest and mature your thoughts for a day or two. Sometimes, a break of as little as five minutes can give you new ideas.

Flow is excellent when you work on the right task. But the right task a little while ago may no longer be the right task. Things change and having flow with the wrong task isn't worth anything. That's why you should switch to the panorama mode at least once an hour and assess your priorities.

The major obstacle on the journey from procrastination to flow is lack of clarity. Unclear prioritization, unclear purpose behind a task, unclear expectations, and unclear feedback loops—these are all obstacles removed by the monotasking method.

DISCRETIONARY TIME WASTE

My client Axel, CEO of a successful startup, told me how he found it hard to get started. Even though he had important tasks on his to-do list, he would reluctantly browse celebrity sites, check the weather forecasts, or play computer games.

Some of your working hours are *hardscaped*, scheduled for meetings or other regularly scheduled, unavoidable tasks. Then there's *discretionary time*. This is when you completely manage yourself, when you typically work with your top priority task. It is easier to waste discretionary time than *non-discretionary time*.

When you attend a meeting, you will always hear some of what is said, however distracted you are. You'll probably also contribute at least a few comments in a discussion. But when you work for yourself, chances are that you do absolutely nothing of what you should do.

Axel and I talked about how he values his discretionary time. He feared that too much of his time was spent in meetings. Although he said he placed a high value on discretionary time, he wasted it. The solution for Axel was to use the concepts of *guilt-free time* and *timeboxing*.

Axel picked the most important task and then set his *panorama cue*. Finally, he just started to focus on that task without having a solution beforehand. When the alarm went off, he now had guilt-free time that he could spend on just about anything.

PROCRASTINATION REASONS AND SYMPTOMS

We plan to do a task, but still we don't do it. Here's a list of typical reasons why we procrastinate:

- **Anticipated criticism:** Sometimes we're afraid to start a task because we think the outcome or the way we do the task may be criticized.
- **Forced by someone:** Someone pushes work on us. It decreases our motivation to get started.
- **Irrelevance for you:** When there's nothing in it for us other tasks get higher priority.
- **Novelty of a task type:** Limited knowledge about a task makes it more diffuse and scarier to start.
- **Stakeholder vacancy:** No one really requested this, but we still have it on our to-do list. Who can answer how to solve this?
- **Success phobia:** We sometimes believe that pressure will increase if we prove that we're competent. We fear that successfully delivering this task will give us more to do in the future.

And here's a list of typical symptoms. Recognizing them makes it easier to know when to act:

- **Beyond our control:** Someone else must do something first.
- **Denial of responsibility:** We claim we're not interested, in order to justify that someone else can do it.
- **Distracting ourselves with trivia:** It makes us feel busy while procrastinating.
- **Motivation absence:** *"Not today, but perhaps tomorrow."*
- **Over-planning:** Pretending we need more information.
- **Passively forgetting:** Letting the mind wander.
- **Trivializing the task:** Saying this task is not important anyway.

All these symptoms are fears. A good way to overcome fear is to expose yourself to what you fear. Find a small next action in this unpleasant task. I can guarantee that you'll feel better when you've started working on it.

WAITER EFFECT

Bluma Zeigarnik noticed that waiters had better recall of orders that had not yet been settled.[105] Numerous experiments have shown that the *waiter effect* is valid.[106] Used correctly, this can help us stop procrastinating and also turn on powerful background problem solving. How?

When a task has been started, cognitive access to the information needed to solve this task is increased. End your working day by writing a note about what to start with tomorrow. This will effectively make your brain start preparing for tomorrow ahead of time.

Our subconscious thinking is unhappy with unfinished tasks, so it keeps disturbing our conscious thinking with reminders to finalize them. It also seems like the importance of the unfinished task makes you remember it better.[107]

As long as tasks are present on our *short list*, they will to some degree be perceived as started and not finished. That's why the short list is limited to five tasks. Never have more than five tasks on today's list and you'll avoid many self-imposed attempts at procrastination.

Cliffhangers in TV series are a deliberate use of the waiter effect. Perhaps the first paragraph of this page made you curious about the rest of this story. You can challenge procrastination by just getting started with a task. Your brain will encourage you to complete it.

THE IVY LEE METHOD

"Show me a way to get more things done," said Charles M. Schwab to Ivy Lee. Schwab, the president of Bethlehem Steel, was constantly looking for methods that would increase his productivity. *"If it works, I'll pay anything within reason,"* he continued.

The renowned management consultant Ivy Lee gave him a blank piece of paper and said: *"Write down the things you have to do tomorrow. Then number these items in the order of their real importance. First thing tomorrow morning, start working on number one."*[108]

Knowledge workers—like you and me—try to solve complex problems. We need simple and general rules to guide us, as each new problem has its own unique challenges. Ivy Lee's method is extremely simple to follow. And it encourages us to monotask.

This method also forces us to make priority decisions: what is really important? We may otherwise be caught by the urgency trap when we arrive at the office tomorrow and something new but actually less important has suddenly appeared.

After a few weeks, Lee received a check for twenty-five thousand dollars—a huge amount at the time. Schwab later said that the *Ivy Lee Method* was the most profitable method he learned throughout his business career. He probably never knew what Maria Ovsiankina discovered.

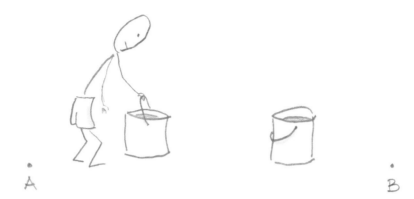

SELF-FULFILLING TASKS

Isn't it a nice feeling to be able to complete your current task before you leave the office? And isn't it sometimes hard to get going in the morning? Minutes ticking away while we engage in trivialities, without really knowing what we should do.

In fact, Maria Ovsiankina's findings in 1928 show that there is a contradiction between completing the task at hand before leaving the office and getting started again the next morning. It is based on Bluma Zeigarnik's discovery in 1927 that we remember interrupted tasks more easily.

Ovsiankina asked her subjects to perform tasks such as folding a paper or translating a text from German to French. During the execution of the task, the subject was interrupted abruptly by, for example, someone dropping things on the floor and asking for help picking them up.

After interruptions as long as fifty minutes, subjects showed a strong willingness to resume the original task, even though they were not asked to do so. We want to finish a task we have started. The desire persists even during breaks.[109]

Ivy Lee's method to write down the most important tasks before leaving the office is a first step to easily getting started the next morning. Simply going home when you are in the middle of a task is even better. A *self-fulfilling task* is an activity that is started, but not completed, before going home. The next day, it *insists* that you complete it.

PRE-CRASTINATION

Pre-crastination is a compulsive tendency to start small and often trivial tasks instantly, even though it might demand more mental or physical effort in the long run. You may think it's a weapon against procrastination, but pre-crastinating is just another type of procrastinating.

Starting at point A, you're asked to pick up one of two buckets on your way to point B and carry it with you to point B. Would you choose the bucket closest to A or to B? Most people choose to carry the near bucket rather than the far bucket, even though they must carry it a longer distance to B.[110]

This is similar to starting the day answering short emails. In the afternoon, you're still struggling with small and even trivial tasks. Spending the whole day on small tasks isn't doing the most important task. In the short term, it's efficiency over effectiveness. Long term, it's not even efficient.

Small wins feel good. We can knock off small, easy tasks quickly. Our brain wants us to complete started tasks.[111] Is a read email a started task that demands a reply to be considered done? The major reason for pre-crastination, though, is the compulsive avoidance of big tasks, however important they are.

Batching of similar tasks saves you setup time. For instance, instead of paying every invoice as soon as it arrives, keep an invoice stack and schedule a weekly invoice paying session. To fight procrastination, it's better to break down tasks that are important as well as big, rather than escape into pre-crastination.

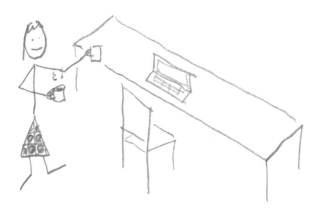

MORNING PROCEDURE

You get to the office with an upcoming project that's so big you don't know where to start. Instead of starting, you escape to the coffee machine for half an hour. Finally, back at your desk, you start browsing aimlessly online and another morning is lost.

What to do? Your personal *morning procedure* is a list you write once and reuse every day. It contains a number of chronologically ordered activities: Activity 1, Activity 2, and so on. Like other checklists, you occasionally modify your morning procedure as you gain new insights.

Here's my morning procedure. Note that this is only an example. You know best what suits you: (1) Remove all papers and things that temporarily reside on my desk. (2) Write down important tasks off the top of my head. (3) Empty my email inbox. (4) Pick one task. (5) Set my panorama cue. (6) Start first mono-tasking session.

New habit: Sit down at your desk as soon as you arrive at the office and set your alarm to the next vertical formation of the minute hand (8:00, 8:30, 9:00, etc.), but not for less than twenty-five minutes. Follow your morning procedure until the alarm sounds.

Your morning procedure starts your inspiration engine. Once you get up to speed, it doesn't require much energy to keep the pace. Following your morning procedure every day will transform it from an extrinsic routine to a habit.

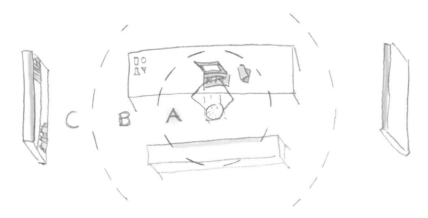

FINGERTIP MANAGEMENT

Fingertip management is a building block in Charles Hobbs's Time Power system.[112] It's having at your fingertips what is needed, when it's needed. Think of your desk as the bullseye in a target with three circular areas labeled A, B, and C.

Area A is what you can reach easily while seated. Here you keep only papers, gadgets, or pens needed for your current monotask. To access Area B, you must stand or stretch. This is where you have things you expect to need today.

Everything else must be in Area C. That is out of sight or some place you must take steps to reach. It's a challenge to put away things we love, care about, and have a sense that we'll use. But that's the point. We deliberately visualize our consciously aware priorities.

Magazines you want to read, interesting books you've bought, and printed documents you've been told to read—either they are a part of today's short list or they should be archived. Archiving is putting them in a drawer, a bookshelf, or, might I say, the trash can.

Fingertip management is similar to the French *mise en place*[113] in the professional kitchen and the Japanese *5S*[114] in manufacturing. Make it a habit to practice fingertip management. Dedicate two or three moments a day to prepare your A, B, and C areas.

PROPER EXECUTION

A common source of procrastination is a frightening feeling that the end result won't be good enough. You can't see the road to the shining result. Even worse, you can't see where the road begins. The solution is to focus on the execution of the task rather than on the end result.

World precision shooting champion Christina Bengtsson ignores the score during practice: *"Shot after shot is fired as perfect as possible, with a towel covering the electronic scoreboard."*[115] The aim is to focus all attention on proper execution rather than on the final score.

Can we make sure we're not wasting time on a less important task if we ignore the end result? That's what our panorama session is for. Prioritizing and focusing simply can't be done at the same time. Therefore, we focus during the monotask session and prioritize during the panorama session.

Monotasking is a method that allows the goal and the execution to evolve with changing conditions. Instead of speculatively nailing down a roadmap towards a faraway but detailed goal, we monotask for a while in the direction we believe in right now. At least once an hour, we evaluate our actual results and adjust our direction.

Choose the most important thing to do right now. Then, set your *panorama cue*. Forget the panorama for a moment and zoom into the task you chose and focus on just doing.

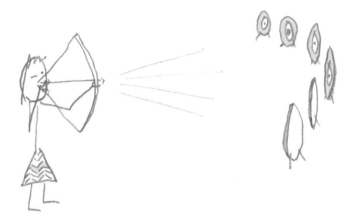

SINGLE GOAL FOCUS

Procrastination is the gap between intentions and action. This gap may shrink when we make our actions more concrete. When we break large tasks down into smaller tasks, we make it more obvious how they are to be performed. Just be aware that *too many* tasks can also lead to procrastination.

The reason that planning a task increases our motivation is precisely that it diminishes our commitment to all other tasks. When we plan too many tasks in detail, none of them seem important. They are concrete, but there are too many for any one task to stand out.

Our task commitment is undermined when we see conflicts between goals or when our anticipated probability of achieving a goal is low. To plan and break down too many tasks makes it clear that our resources of time, attention, and energy are limited.[116]

Creating goals should not be seen as an isolated task. Rather, it is a complex system in which individual goals are interrelated. Most tasks remain undone in overly long to-do lists, not only because there are too many tasks but also because the very length of the list undermines our commitment.

The *short list*, limited to five tasks, and the weekly *weeding* of our *grass catcher list*, reduces the number of tasks that the *waiter effect* can disturb us with. Monotasking successfully also demands that you avoid breaking down other tasks than the one you're working on right now.

HARDSCAPE PROCRASTINATION

As we noted earlier, research has shown that people expect to have more slack time in the future than they do in the present.[117] Interestingly, this even applies to tasks we would enjoy with immediate benefits. In particular, we procrastinate even more when opportunities have a distant expiration date.

Suzanne B. Shu and Ayelet Gneezy studied this.[118] They showed that travelers who have visited a city for two weeks have seen significantly more landmarks than the average resident who has lived there for one year or more. If we know we'll stay for a year in Paris, it's not as important to visit the Eiffel Tower today.

Shu and Gneezy also distributed two types of gift certificates good for a slice of cake and a beverage at a high-quality local French pastry café. The first group got certificates that would expire in three weeks. The second group got certificates expiring in three months.

At the time of receiving the certificates, the group with certificates with further out expiration dates were much more confident that they would redeem them. In reality, those who received certificates with a close expiration date were five times as likely to redeem them as those in the long expiration date group.

Visiting landmarks and cafés are hardscapes. Either these tasks aren't important enough to be performed or they should promptly be scheduled in our calendar. That decision had to be made as soon as the gift certificates were received. Otherwise, cake eating won't happen.

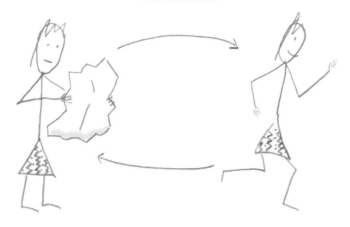

THE OVER-PLANNER'S PROCRASTINATION

Spending too much time up front on planning is procrastination. You plan the work, but you don't work the plan. The reason may be that the outcome of a big task is diffuse. Or that a new type of task makes you worried about whether others will appreciate or devalue your work.

Isaac Newton wrote in the definition of *inertia* that bodies will preserve their present state, whether at rest or moving.[119] Translated into psychology, Maria Ovsiankina showed that if we just start a task, then we'll feel a strong desire to continue and finish it.[120]

You face a big task. Planning everything upfront doesn't mean the task is moving. As long as the work is at rest, we'll feel resistance to carrying out the plan. The *waiter effect* keeps the task we're planning present in our mind,[121] but we won't get any result until we work the plan.

Over-planning is speculative. After completing 20 percent of a big detailed plan, we may find that we want to change the focus of our work. In that case, planning the remaining 80 percent ahead of time would be a waste. Instead, we can get hints on how to proceed by just getting started.

Think about the purpose of this task. What would make stakeholders more effective? Planning the next action step is the most effortless strategy to get the task moving. Work that plan and after that, get feedback from others. Now it's easy to maintain the velocity.

REFLEXIVE VS. REFLECTIVE THINKING

Consider a model where two thinking machines run in parallel in the brain. They cooperate and send information to each other. We can call them System 1 and System 2.[122]

- **System 1** is in charge of rapid and automatic thinking. It's reflexive, sometimes a little bit crazy, and it doesn't need much energy. On the other hand, it ignores our self-control. We hear someone call our name and turn our head. System 1 did it automatically and without cognitive effort.
- **System 2** controls our thoughts and behaviors. It's reflective and evaluates clever as well as crazy ideas sent from System 1. Then System 2 makes the final decision and chooses where we should put our attention. The capacity of System 2 is limited by our small working memory.

Our ability to focus attention on a task depends very much on the condition of System 2. Most often, we need self-control. However, our reflective thinking is easily overloaded. Because of its lazy nature, too many stimuli make System 2 give up all its ambitions. Beeping notifications from your smartphone impair your ability to control your attention and keep it focused on the most important task.

People who are cognitively busy also make selfish choices, superficial judgments, and use offensive language.[123] You sit at home and try to focus on writing an important business letter while the children are noisily playing. Suddenly you are uncontrollably yelling at them.

CLUTTER

Hoarding is a serious disease that can make people completely fill their space and time with useless collectibles. Even if you are not an unhealthy collector, it may be good to know that office clutter can both decrease your productivity and perhaps increase your creativity.

Kathleen Vohs and her colleagues conducted some interesting experiments on this. Participants were asked to list ten new applications for ping pong balls. The test results showed that people in a messy room did better than those in a neat room.

In another of her experiments, people in a messy room more often chose a product labeled *new* over one labeled *classic*. An orderly environment appears to activate a mindset to follow conventions, while the disordered environment motivates you to try new things.[124]

However, there is also research supporting that irrelevant and peripheral visual stimuli steals your attention.[125] That's validated by many people's experience: it's hard to focus on your task when you have many and varied sounds around you.

Your messy desk boosts procrastination because you always have something trivial such as cleaning or sorting right there. It grabs your attention, and might make you think that you should do that first.

To stay productive, keep your desk clear of clutter. Paper and other things that have remained untouched for two weeks must be removed—no matter how interesting or useful they appear. When it comes to workshops or hatching new ideas, a café environment or a walk outdoors is preferable to a messy work environment.

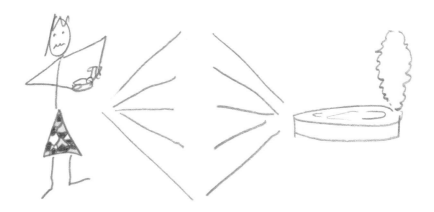

WICKED PROBLEM

You're dealing with an ill-formulated problem. The information is confusing. There are many clients and decision makers. And unfortunately, they all have conflicting priorities. Faced with a *wicked problem*, design thinking might be more helpful than analytical thinking.[126]

While analytical thinking makes controlled experiments in the natural world and values objectivity, design thinking models and synthesizes a future world that may be more practical.[127] Analysts wonder if it's true. Designers wonder if it will be usable.

In design thinking, formulating the problem is part of the method. For example, start with the problem of how to open canned tuna. Opening it with a can opener works, but we ponder whether we can open the can in a more appropriate and practical way. It may not involve a traditional can opener.

All design is re-design. You start with something that already exists and then either compose or improvise a new thing. Solving this kind of constructed problem is often very fun and engaging. Iteratively, you break things down and then put them together in a new, never-before-seen way.

Stanford University developed a design-thinking method with the following flow: empathize, define, ideate, prototype, and test.[128] Every iteration starts with divergent thinking, seeking variety, and continues with convergent thinking, testing new combinations.

VISUALIZE BEFORE YOU START

Visualizing sometimes helps overcome procrastination when starting a big task. This is not about creating a detailed project charter in order to lock in cost, quality, and time—the Barnes triangle[129]—up front. Rather, it's an analysis, where the outcome is your gained knowledge.

1. Start by writing down the impact that you want to create. The impact isn't the artifact you create, like a sales report. The impact of writing the sales report may be to give the managers a usable basis for decision making for their product management.

2. Put the most important impact from (1) in the middle of a new mind map.[130] Along the spokes add roles and persons associated with the impact. Who will benefit from this impact? Who's got crucial information that can help you? Who's the sponsor?

3. Look at the mind map from (2) and ponder a minimum viable idea you could verify in a narrow time. Connected to this impact, what could you do right now and show other people to get feedback? You're not looking for praise, just second opinions.

Note that the minimum viable idea doesn't have to solve the whole problem or create the impact. The outstanding purpose is to learn. Is this the right way toward the solution? What could be the next small step along this road? Will this help the stakeholders?

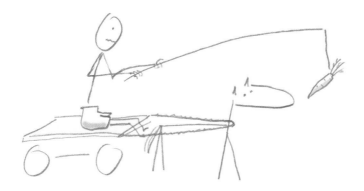

INTRINSIC MOTIVATION

As long as we do mechanical, repetitive tasks, we're motivated by incentives. But when it comes to tasks that require creative thinking, rewards and punishment actually lead to worse performance.[131] Autonomy, mastery, and purpose motivate us to solve complex problems.

- **Autonomy** emerges when you have a sense of volition and choice in how to use your time, tasks, and tools. We are wired to be active and engaged. Autonomy is not a synonym for independence. Rather, it means that you are empowered to do your tasks in the way you believe is best.
- **Mastery** is the mindset that there is always room for improvement. You can develop all your skills—poor and exceptional. It demands effort and deliberate practice from you. With mastery, you'll sometimes experience the wonderful feeling of flow. Challenges match your abilities perfectly.
- **Purpose**—a reason to be happy—is a stronger driver than happiness itself.[132] You want to do tasks that matter. You want to do them well. And you want to be a part of something bigger than yourself. A good purpose often maximizes your reward, not the other way around.

Daniel Pink's book *Drive* is a convincing explanation of why *intrinsic motivation* is superior to extrinsic motivation.[133] This is not a question exclusively for those in management. You can fight procrastination by striving to strengthen your autonomy, mastery, and purpose at work.

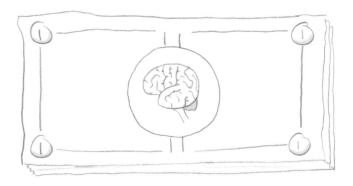

BRAIN ECONOMY

Many office workers unfortunately end up with days like this: Mornings are accidentally spent on trivialities, sometimes not even job related. Tedious tasks are pushed to the afternoon. But, in the afternoon, your brain starts running low on resources. You suffer from *ego depletion*.

The prefrontal cortex is the most modern brain component in our human evolution. It is the one that allows us to imagine things that don't yet exist. That's fabulous, but we must be aware that it's more energy intensive than the older and simpler parts of the brain. Prioritizing is exhausting.[134]

Choosing what to do today—what to prioritize—is hard work for the prefrontal cortex. We have to think about results that are not yet available and compare their respective values. Because our brain energy level is maximal in the morning,[135] mornings are the best time to plan the day and prioritize tasks.[136]

You'll learn new things during the day, and you must leave the possibility to reprioritize open. That will be easier when you start the day by limiting the selectable tasks to five items. You write them on your short list. In the morning, you still have the brain economy to select correctly.

Finally, you choose the most important task from your short list. It's for your first monotasking session. Don't avoid difficult or inconvenient tasks. It's now, in the morning, that you have the energy to eat the ugliest frog. And that will give you self-confidence for the rest of the day.[137]

NEVER PROCRASTINATE – SUMMARY

Q: I start every morning with a clear intention to complete a particular task. For some reason I don't get started and in the afternoon I'm too tired. What can I do?

A: Planning and prioritizing largely takes place in the part of the brain called the *prefrontal cortex*. It's an energy thirsty organ and it may run out of fuel if you delay planning and prioritizing until the afternoon. The best way to get started immediately in the morning is to leave the office the day before in the middle of a task. Our brain has a strong willingness to resume what we have already started.

Q: When I start a new task, I usually make detailed plans of all steps upfront. I want to make sure that I don't make any mistakes. Then I usually run out of time. Why?

A: Over-planning is not only a typical symptom of escape to procrastination but it also reduces your motivation to complete the task. Planning a task diminishes your commitment to all other tasks. Planning too many subtasks in detail makes them all seem less important. Seeing all the steps needed might make you feel that it will be difficult to succeed. Your commitment to the task is undermined.

Q: I'm a notorious over-committer. Why do I always accept too many requests?

A: It's the nature of our brains to expect more slack time in the future than we have in the present. Distant deadlines seem easy to meet, and this can encourage us to take on more than we can manage. It's called *time inconsistency* when we have one intention when planning up front but change our mind when it's time to do the task. The treatment is to make space for slack in your planning and clearly say *"no"* when you know you won't do a task anyway.

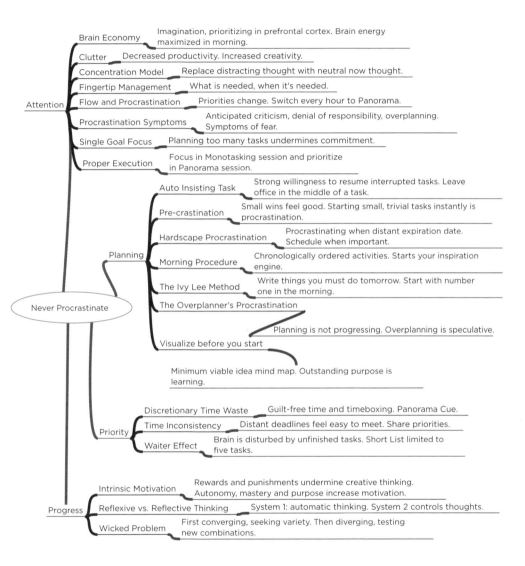

Never Procrastinate

Attention
- Brain Economy — Imagination, prioritizing in prefrontal cortex. Brain energy maximized in morning.
- Clutter — Decreased productivity. Increased creativity.
- Concentration Model — Replace distracting thought with neutral now thought.
- Fingertip Management — What is needed, when it's needed.
- Flow and Procrastination — Priorities change. Switch every hour to Panorama.
- Procrastination Symptoms — Anticipated criticism, denial of responsibility, overplanning. Symptoms of fear.
- Single Goal Focus — Planning too many tasks undermines commitment.
- Proper Execution — Focus in Monotasking session and prioritize in Panorama session.

Planning
- Auto Insisting Task — Strong willingness to resume interrupted tasks. Leave office in the middle of a task.
- Pre-crastination — Small wins feel good. Starting small, trivial tasks instantly is procrastination.
- Hardscape Procrastination — Procrastinating when distant expiration date. Schedule when important.
- Morning Procedure — Chronologically ordered activities. Starts your inspiration engine.
- The Ivy Lee Method — Write things you must do tomorrow. Start with number one in the morning.
- The Overplanner's Procrastination — Planning is not progressing. Overplanning is speculative.
- Visualize before you start — Minimum viable idea mind map. Outstanding purpose is learning.

Priority
- Discretionary Time Waste — Guilt-free time and timeboxing. Panorama Cue.
- Time Inconsistency — Distant deadlines feel easy to meet. Share priorities.
- Waiter Effect — Brain is disturbed by unfinished tasks. Short List limited to five tasks.

Progress
- Intrinsic Motivation — Rewards and punishments undermine creative thinking. Autonomy, mastery and purpose increase motivation.
- Reflexive vs. Reflective Thinking — System 1: automatic thinking. System 2 controls thoughts.
- Wicked Problem — First converging, seeking variety. Then diverging, testing new combinations.

CHAPTER 5
PROGRESS INCREMENTALLY

IT'S NOT ENOUGH TO do the thing right if we don't do the right thing. However, everything changes, even what's seen as the right thing. We may have misunderstood our stakeholders, they may have changed their mind, or we may have a new and smarter idea.

We must synchronize our goals frequently with our stakeholders. While working on a task, we'll learn new things. When we see our results, the stakeholders will learn new things. Sometimes this new knowledge leads us to change our priorities.

This chapter emphasizes the value of embracing change. We must break down our tasks, do a little and then show our results to our stakeholders. *Timeboxing* combined with *Lakein's question* ensures that we use our most up-to-date knowledge.

IN ONE MINUTE: HOW TO PROGRESS INCREMENTALLY

Five simple concepts:

- **Task breakdown** is probably the most effective way to fight procrastination. It's easier to get started with a small task than a big one. Never forget the purpose of the big task though. And don't make detailed plans upfront for every possible subtask.
- **Lakein's question** is *"What's the best use of my time right now?"* It's the question we must ask ourselves frequently. Inspecting our results to this point, considering our answer to Lakein's question, and adapting our plan is mandatory when we want to be effective.
- **Timeboxing** is when we decide upfront when to start, when to stop, and what task to focus on. It's not about size or quality of the outcome. It's purely about attention. But, of course, there's a correlation between successful focus and productivity.
- **Push the fledgling out of the nest** by exposing our ideas and our results early. We do this in order to get feedback. The feedback helps us adjust the next action step in the best direction. Here's what I've done, what's the best way to proceed?
- **Faked Urgency** is a duplicitous trick to make you put effort into less important tasks. Tasks that set you in reactive mode—but when examined objectively aren't important—are a waste. They keep you busy and impede the real work.

Questionnaire:

In order to kickstart your neurons, put a checkmark next to every statement below that you consider to be a recurring time robber in your current workplace.

- ☐ Incomplete work
- ☐ Changing requirements
- ☐ No stakeholders available
- ☐ Tight deadlines
- ☐ Faked urgency
- ☐ Repeating the same mistakes
- ☐ Waiting for people
- ☐ Impromptu tasks
- ☐ Failure to delegate
- ☐ Everyday administration
- ☐ Too many levels of decision makers
- ☐ Micromanagement of delegated tasks
- ☐ Attempting to do too much at once
- ☐ Deadlines
- ☐ Snap decisions
- ☐ Lack of feedback
- ☐ Moving from crisis to crisis
- ☐ One person is a bottleneck for many others
- ☐ Bureaucracy impediments
- ☐ Long-term planning

A CUCUMBER AND AN ARTICHOKE MEET FOR A WALK IN THE FOREST

Cucumber: Long time no see, Art. What's new?

Artichoke: I've worked hard this month. I made a huge delivery to a customer.

Cucumber: Were they satisfied with what you delivered?

Artichoke: Unfortunately, no.

Cucumber: Why?

Artichoke: I don't really understand. I delivered exactly what they ordered. Yet, they now say they want something else.

Cucumber: Isn't it natural to get new insights when you see what you ordered?

Artichoke: Yes, I suppose you're right. I should have coordinated with them early to find out if they liked what I had started.

Cucumber: What would have happened if they changed their minds at that moment?

Artichoke: I could have shifted focus without wasting too much time.

Cucumber: It's like you make a bet when you order something: I think I want this in the future. If you order something big, it's a big risk.

Artichoke: You're right. Working in smaller increments with the ability to adapt after a while reduces risks.

TASK BREAKDOWN

Tasks that are too big might be the number one reason for procrastination. How do you eat an elephant? After the first bite, the *waiter effect* will help us keep the pace.[138] Unfortunately, *task breakdown* still fails too often. One of the reasons is that we break down tasks as a detailed roadmap: from start to goal.

Before breaking down your task, start with the higher purpose of it. Determine whether and why you should spend time on this task and not on another arbitrary task. In what way will the world be a better place when you deliver the final result? One or two sentences is enough here.

Step two is to write down a list of stakeholders and why each one wants you to do this task. Stakeholders may be those who directly use your result, such as people reading your report. Also, those who pay and those who are indirectly affected by your results are stakeholders.

The third step is to find one to five small tasks that will result in feedback. For example, the list could include locating previous reports, writing headlines, or contacting someone who can give you valuable information. You'll gain more knowledge about the main task by doing these smaller subtasks.

When you've completed the small tasks on your *short list* but not the main task, share the results with others, reassess the higher purpose, and finally find one to five new small tasks. You now take advantage of the knowledge you won while working on this task.

LAKEIN'S QUESTION

There are many excuses to not do the most important thing right now: someone just asked me to do a thing, I promised to do a thing a long time ago, I am eager to do a thing, I have a looming deadline. I'm sure you can think of others. But is this thing the best use of my time right now?

Alan Lakein coined *Lakein's question*[139] in the 1970s:

- What's the best use of my time right now?

He urged us to ask the question when we're in doubt about what to do. And when we're distracted. And when we procrastinate. And when it generally feels natural. In the monotasking method, we ask Lakein's question at least once an hour.

The thing that was most important a moment ago may not be so right now. The financial report you began to write this morning isn't completed at 11 a.m. However, during your 11 a.m. panorama, you realize you have to send an invoice before lunch. Now, the answer to Lakein's question is: invoice.

As we already discussed, there's a cost attached to task switching. That's why monotasking is a great help for those who want to accomplish something in a world with more and more demands for attention. Nonetheless, doing the most important thing must overshadow all other priority strategies.

Monotasking does not force you to say *"no"* to new tasks. By asking Lakein's question at least once an hour, during your *panorama session*, and focusing in between on one and only one task—the most important one right now—you will simultaneously maximize your flexibility and effectiveness.

BUILD, MEASURE, LEARN

In addition to changing priorities, you may also have to deal with changing expectations or desired outcomes. The task you committed to is pre-specified in detail, in terms of delivery dates, methods, and outcome. You follow the specification. Still, the receiver doesn't feel like there is any value in the final delivered product. Build, measure, learn[140] reduces the risk of working for a long time in the wrong direction.

On day one of a project, you have a set of hypotheses or guesses about what you should do to meet the stakeholder's needs. To build means in this context that you want to test your hypotheses in the simplest possible way. Create something to get a reaction that gives you more knowledge.

It's not necessarily about making a prototype or delivering intermittent results. You can, for example, make a presentation, show it to others and get feedback. The presentation may describe your activities, qualities in what you will deliver, or what benefits the target group will get.

Use the feedback you get to confirm your hypotheses or draw new conclusions. Your findings will show that some hypotheses are correct, and some must be rejected. The new knowledge inspires you to create new hypotheses. You test them in a second iteration. Your outcome is moving incrementally.

Further ideas are tested, iteration after iteration. In this way, the outcome you construct is anchored in reality. Stakeholders who have opportunities to see firsthand what they'll receive will give you better guidance on what they want. They can influence the direction early with build, measure, learn.

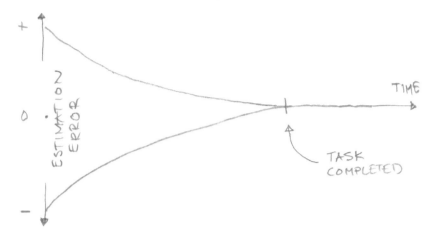

CONE OF UNCERTAINTY

The client wants to know when you'll deliver. You don't know, but you guess: in three days. Unsatisfied, the customer says that's too late. You don't want to lie, but you want the client to be happy with your answer, and you want to manage the risk of not meeting your estimates. How?

Hofstadter's law claims that tasks will always take longer than you expect, even when you take into account Hofstadter's law.[141] Although self-referential in a crazy way, it hints at something important: tasks that require thinking can't possibly be estimated 100 percent accurately in advance.

Solving a problem involves making numerous small decisions and stepwise seeing progress you couldn't predict. If there were no decisions and all progress was predictable, then it wouldn't have been a problem in the first place.

Question: At what point is it easiest to estimate the time required to complete a task? Answer: At the point when we have completed this task. This law about the lack of accuracy in predicting the outcome in knowledge work is referred to as the *cone of uncertainty*.[142]

Making the client continuously aware of your progress allows her to be involved in the estimation process. Instead of promising delivery in three days, promise to focus on the task for one day and then show her your progress. At that point, you'll both have a better understanding of the time needed to accomplish the task.

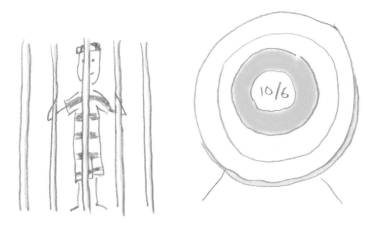

DEADLINES, TARGET DATES, AND DUE DATES

Deadlines and target dates are not the same. It's crucial to be careful when you use these terms, especially with managers or customers. Mixing them arbitrarily gives people unrealistic expectations. This creates poor prioritization, anger, and in the worst case, missed business opportunities.

U.S. prisons in 19th century were surrounded by stockades and if prisoners passed that perimeter, they were shot dead. Hence, it was called a *deadline*.[143] The newspapers took up this term to mean the time when you had to deliver a text to get it in the next paper before it went to print.

In our modern office world, missing a deadline implies there's no point doing anything more on this task. Preparing a presentation for a meeting has a deadline. There's no point changing the presentation after the meeting.

A *target date* is not a deadline. It's an expected date for a defined delivery. It might have been communicated to others. Missing the target date may have negative consequences, but it's still reasonable to go on to complete this task. A *due date* is similar to a target date.

Self-imposed target dates decrease procrastination,[144] probably because you are able to benefit from a constructed sense of urgency. However, this is a counterproductive way of tricking yourself. Prioritizing must be based on importance, not urgency.

TIMEBOXING

Rather than deadlines and target dates, we use *timeboxing* in the monotasking method. We want to be able to be flexible in prioritizing our discretionary time based on our most recent knowledge. Otherwise we can't maximize the effective value of what we do.

In timeboxing, we set three parameters in advance: when to start the timebox, when to stop the timebox, and what task we'll focus on. A successful timebox is thus a period when we start at the expected time, stop at the expected time, and focus on nothing other than the chosen task.

This is a totally different way of thinking. In timeboxing, we focus on focus instead of focusing on the result. Regardless of quality and quantity of the result, we're happy if we manage to monotask on the most important thing.

A timebox might happen to be smaller than the task. That's no problem. In the *panorama session*, before your next timebox, you've got the power to decide whether you'll spend one more timebox on this task or switch to another one. The flexible prioritization in timeboxing makes it less risky than deadlines.

Why is timeboxing better and less risky than deadlines? Because we're not concerned with things beyond our control. You can control what you focus on and when to stop. But you can't decide, before you've even started, that you'll successfully complete this task before the deadline.

FAKED URGENCY

Urgency is the marketer's best friend. In order to sell something to you, he wants you to have a sense of urgency. Urgency makes us act. Therefore, it's good to recognize when tasks only seem to be urgent. There are a number of ways this can happen:

- **Opportunity lost urgency:** Asked to act within a time frame, you should always think about the worst-case scenario. What will happen if I don't act? Probably nothing terrible.
- **Hard achievement urgency:** When people tell you this task is a tough one, they might lean on Festinger's effort justification paradigm, which states that we tend to value outcomes that required more effort to achieve.[145]
- **Competition urgency:** Act now or otherwise you will lose this game. But what if the game is not important? When you spend time on extraneous competitions, you win battles while losing the war.
- **Scarcity urgency:** Research shows that we act when a resource appears to be limited.[146] This applies, for instance, when you're offered responsibility for a task and not taking it means this meritorious job will be given to your colleague.
- **Time-words urgency:** Be aware when words like *now*, *quick*, *rapid*, and *instant* are a part of the task description. They might be there just to give you a false sense of urgency.

The monotasker prioritizes tasks based on importance, not urgency. Tasks that put you in reactive mode—but when examined objectively aren't important—are waste. They keep you busy and impede the real work.

MANAGEMENT BY CRISIS

Staff is shuffled, an upcoming date is repeated incessantly, and potential heroes are identified. Do you recognize this? Management communicates that the organization is threatened, that there's an element of surprise, and that there isn't enough time to make reasonable decisions.

Let me say first that a project or a task is never late. We may have had unrealistic expectations of what we would achieve until today. But right now, when we know what we have completed, we shouldn't be influenced by what we believed in the past. Failed plans are history.

Remain calm when the light of crisis is flashing. Start by analyzing the current situation. Where am I right now? Develop relevant assumptions. Will the current conditions continue to exist within the time span of the failed plan you've committed to?[147] If yes, shred the old plan.

Based on where you are, establish new objectives. What do you want to achieve? Are there alternative paths to these objectives? Try to disregard the option to spend too much time in the office. It's rarely effective. With no rest, your pace slows down. Overall, you'll achieve less.

Because his performance doesn't match his expectations, a long-distance runner who sprints continuously won't complete the entire distance. Widening the perspectives makes it clear that we maximize our long-term productivity when we keep a sustainable pace.

OPERACY

Edward de Bono said that it's a particularly silly aspect of culture that separates thinkers from doers.[148] He coined the term *operacy* to represent the thinking involved in doing or the skill needed for doing. Operacy is based on simplicity, practicality, and effectiveness.[149]

- **Is the task simple enough?** The idea of simple initiatives refers to doing the obvious. We come up with a smart idea, implement it quickly, and learn while doing. To succeed, we must have a tolerance for error and failure. By doing simple things, we've got time and space to reorient and continue with what works.
- **Is the task doable?** Is it realistic that doing this simple task will give us more knowledge on how to proceed? Always think about the most likely outcome before prioritizing a task. The most likely outcome is not necessarily the same as the desired outcome.
- **Is the task effective?** Efficiency is about balancing input and output. Effectiveness is about setting up for the result you want. Operacy is about doing the things that matter. You prioritize the most effective step right now.

In the real world, there are people, plans, conflicts, trade-offs, and agreements. You must assess the situation and then act on your own initiative. Doing without thinking is not enough. Neither is thinking without doing. Operacy is street smartness that accomplishes things.

PUSH THE FLEDGLING OUT OF THE NEST

You've got everything to gain from sharing your minimal viable idea. Explain it to your colleagues during a coffee break, or in metaphoric terms to your family at home. Even dumb questions and harsh criticism can help you develop your work one step further.

Incremental development is superior to making big plans up front. Do a little work, demonstrate it to others, get some feedback, and adapt. The attitude is transparent, risk-minimizing, and exploratory: here's what I've done, now what's the best way to proceed?

It's the diversity in opinions that improves your work. Nobody is an expert in everything, but the errors in each of their suggestions may cancel out until only useful information is left.[150] Respect people who take the time to share their opinions with you and be grateful for all feedback. It's their true experience, regardless of whether it's absolute truth.

And what goes around, comes around. Research has found that when employees hide knowledge, they trigger a reciprocal distrust loop in which coworkers are unwilling to share knowledge in return.[151] Sharing early work is a great way to build long-term trust.

Don't just look for praise. Negative criticism and apparent misunderstandings can accelerate the process of re-orienting on your goals, if you use it correctly. You should analyze what they don't understand and why, then figure out how you can clarify. Also, ask them how they would tweak your work.

PARKINSON'S LAW

"It is a commonplace observation that work expands so as to fill the time available for its completion. Thus, an elderly lady of leisure can spend an entire day in writing and dispatching a postcard to her niece at Bognor Regis."

Northcote Parkinson wrote these words in 1955 and named it *Parkinson's law*.[152] Assigning a task to a time span in our calendar is always little more than a bet. Not only are we betting on how long the task takes. We're betting that doing this particular task at this particular time is the best use of our time.

Estimating how long a task will take is under the law of natural variation. Sometimes it takes more time than we expected beforehand, sometimes less. Parkinson's law kicks in when the task is completed quickly and instead of moving on to the next task, we simply waste the remaining blocked out time.

What if you reduce the stake? *Timeboxing* makes you more flexible. When the time is up, you assess whether the current task needs more time, or you want to go on with another task. The monotasking solution to Parkinson's law is thus to reprioritize frequently.

The biggest waste of productivity, however, is following an outdated plan when your new knowledge says that this is no longer the most important task. You've scheduled yourself to work on task A now. But a more important task B appears after you made this plan. Go ahead and skip A.

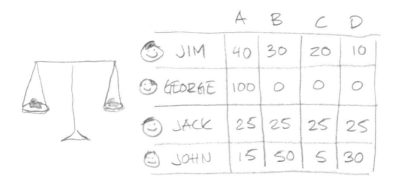

		A	B	C	D
😊	JIM	40	30	20	10
😊	GEORGE	100	0	0	0
😊	JACK	25	25	25	25
😊	JOHN	15	50	5	30

KINDS OF PRIORITY

Differentiating between the various kinds of priority is not just hair-splitting. That's what Dickerson W. Hogue wrote in 1970.[153] He laid out four different kinds of perceived priority using as an example the case of four businessmen who think they have agreed that project A is top-priority, B next, C next, then D. However . . .

- **Relative priority:** Jim felt that all four projects should be worked on simultaneously, but with more effort put on higher priority projects.
- **Spillover priority:** George felt that all available effort should be put on the top priority project until it was completed. Only spillover time is spent on the next highest project.
- **In-case-of-conflict priority:** Jack felt that all projects should be worked on simultaneously with equal effort unless some type of conflict arises among the projects. In case of conflict, A is favored over the other three.
- **Completion priority:** John felt that the priorities discussed only established the order in which the projects would be completed.

In the monotasking productivity system, we use a flexible version of spillover priority. All available effort should be put on the most important task. However, at least once an hour, we ask ourselves *Lakein's question:*[154] *"What's the best use of my time right now?"*

Things change and we learn all the time. Priorities can change rapidly as well. That's what the *panorama session* is for: to take a look at the current landscape and re-prioritize if necessary. When we've made up our mind and picked one task, there should be no doubt that this particular task is the only one to get attention until the next *panorama cue.*

PROMISE BEHAVIOR!

When we count our chickens before they're hatched, the distance between now and the future is ignored. Unfortunately, promising up front to complete ten big tasks by next week doesn't make them already done.

We don't know now what we'll know in the future. Why pretend that what we've planned to do is already done? When we promise results, negative concepts such as *lack of time*, *time optimist*, and *time pressure* are ever-present. We can avoid them by communicating priorities and exposing progress.

Estimates are only guesses. Don't fallaciously confuse planned hours with progression.[155] You may schedule all your tasks in your calendar, but one task might be vastly harder or more time consuming than you anticipated. We can't know until a task is done how much time it will require.

The farmer who has always had one ox to plow his field cannot count on quadrupling his harvest just because he buys three more oxen. However, nowadays we live in era where what is not yet even born is counted speculatively as a guaranteed future income.[156]

Instead of promising results in advance, promise behavior. Instead of promising to complete task A in a week, promise to give task A high priority and to show after two days how far you've come. Frequent review and adaptation is called incremental work.

PROGRESS INCREMENTALLY – SUMMARY

Q: When in flow, I sometimes spend too much time on minor details. How can I make sure that I don't get stuck in subtasks?

A: The monotasking rhythm is very helpful when you want to spend your time on the most important tasks and still take time to determine whether priorities have changed. Set the *panorama cue* alarm to the next half or full hour (10:00, 10:30, 11:00, etc.) at least twenty-five minutes away, and when the alarm sounds, start your *panorama session* by looking over the potential task landscape. Ask yourself, *"What's the best use of my time right now?"* Bring the most important task to your *monotasking session*. Focus solely on that task until the next panorama cue, when you go back to panorama mode again. This effectively means that you explicitly review your priorities at least every half hour.

Q: It's very hard to estimate work up front and it's even harder to meet deadlines I committed to. Is there a way to make better predictions?

A: Deadlines are big bets: I will complete this before that point in time and it's the best use of my time. This is not a good method because it doesn't consider change and new insights. In the monotasking method, you promise what you can control: behavior instead of outcomes. That's fairer. Promise to focus on this task and give early feedback to stakeholders. The monotasking rhythm helps you frequently see where you are and decide on the best next step.

Q: What's the best way to break down tasks?

A: Parkinson's law tells us that work expands to fill the time we assign for it. In monotasking, we assign small slices of time to a task or its subtasks, which are smaller and require less time than the time necessary to complete the full task. The breaks in between these slices are great opportunities to adjust the final goals for this task and sometimes even discover that the task is actually good enough now. The best way to break down the task is to start with something that gives us feedback, something we can show to others, or something that gives us new insights.

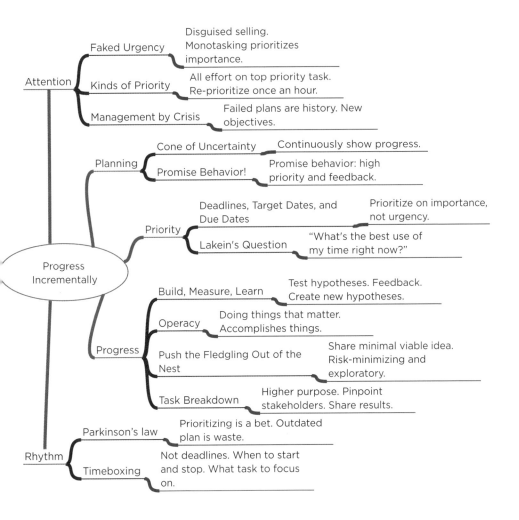

CHAPTER 6
SIMPLIFY COOPERATION

EVEN FROM A STRICTLY personal perspective on productivity, cooperating smoothly with others is crucial. You rarely work on something that doesn't involve anyone else as a supplier, receiver, beneficiary, or other kind of stakeholder.

An abundance mentality is the key skill to save you from anxiety, anger, and redundant work when you work in cooperation with others. Effective communication gives you more discretionary time by eliminating the need for excessive follow-ups and clarifications. Constructively addressing potential disagreements ahead of time also paves the way for the best solution to be implemented.

This chapter presents many pragmatic and easily implemented practices for improved cooperation in recurring office situations, such as making a phone call, listening effectively, and responding to meeting invitations. Performing your own tasks isn't enough if you don't cooperate well with colleagues.

IN ONE MINUTE: HOW TO SIMPLIFY COOPERATION

Five simple concepts:

- **Abundance mentality** is when you share time, knowledge, and connections with colleagues. It'll not only improve your colleagues' work, but they will also be willing to share back.[157] Recognizing all your available options leads the way to win-win solutions.

- **Relationship responsibility** belongs to each one of us. We must understand that the other people in our office are as much individuals as we are. If we can learn about their strengths and weaknesses, we will benefit more from our cooperative efforts.

- **Effective meetings** require that you don't just routinely accept all invitations. Is there a limited purpose for this meeting? Will your contribution matter? Neither should you invite others to meetings without clearly describing your sole purpose.

- **Deliberative rhetoric** is the future-looking and most creative way of discussing something. Never blame others for events in the past and don't get stuck in debates on core values. It's more constructive to think about ways to move on from where you are now.

- **Transparency** forces us to practice what we preach. And if we still get trapped in *cognitive dissonance*, we must step back, look around with an open mind, and suggest a new route that is win-win for everybody.

Questionnaire:

In order to kickstart your neurons, put a checkmark next to every statement below that you consider to be a recurring time robber in your current workplace.

- ☐ Blame games
- ☐ Unreliable colleagues
- ☐ Scarcity mentality
- ☐ Unfocused meetings
- ☐ Estimates interpreted as promises
- ☐ Important tasks outside of everyone's responsibility
- ☐ Long lasting email discussions
- ☐ Noisy colleagues
- ☐ Poorly done jobs that must be done over
- ☐ Incomplete information

- ☐ Disorganization
- ☐ Failure to listen
- ☐ Doing it yourself
- ☐ Seized empowerment
- ☐ Fragile communication channels
- ☐ Waiting for people
- ☐ Indecision and deferred decisions
- ☐ Too many people involved in trivial decisions
- ☐ Lack of commitment from technical experts
- ☐ Unqualified manpower

A CUCUMBER AND AN ARTICHOKE MEET AT THE PIAZZA

Cucumber: How's life, Artie?

Artichoke: Not bad. Besides the fact that I facilitated a terrible meeting today.

Cucumber: What kind of meeting was it?

Artichoke: We have a regular biweekly debriefing. I'm the project manager. Only two of the people I invited showed up.

Cucumber: How many did you invite?

Artichoke: I always invite all eighteen project members. I let them present their status reports, one by one.

Cucumber: Oh. It sounds like a long meeting.

Artichoke: The first meeting, where almost everyone showed up, took three and a half hours.

Cucumber: Are they interested in each other's reports?

Artichoke: No, not really. They work in different areas. Maybe I should organize more meetings with fewer participants.

Cucumber: That sounds like a good idea. You might even hold them more frequently.

Artichoke: Yes. Then they'll certainly be shorter and more relevant.

ABUNDANCE MENTALITY

Yessica's inconvenience wasn't only that she unexpectedly didn't get promoted. The fact that Nicolle was rewarded with the position Yessica was hoping for made her even angrier. The scarcity mentality is the zero-sum paradigm of life.[158] Yessica believes that she can only win if someone else loses.

If you do experience a letdown or disappointment, don't magnify the negative implications. Concentrate your thinking on what you can do right now to make your life better. The *abundance mentality* means taking responsibility over your life. It makes you feel free. Past failures will come to seem far less significant.

The opposite of abundance is scarcity. People who embrace a scarcity mentality believe recognition, opportunity, and other resources are limited. They protect what they have and all that matters is how they compare to others. It prevents them from seeing opportunities and puts them under pressure.

The scarcity mentality makes us focus not only on our own position and resources but also on other people's failures. That is counterproductive, since we can only control our own actions. We should recognize all options rather than just go for the default. Seeking win-win solutions and situations will reward us.

Instead of trying to win an argument, listen with empathy and seek consensus. The only one you should compete with is yourself. Share time, knowledge, and connections with your colleagues. You'll not only help your colleagues grow and improve but they will also be willing to share back.[159]

LUCK FACTOR

Richard Wiseman identified four principles that lucky people practice: 1) creating, noticing, and acting upon opportunities; 2) listening to intuition; 3) practicing optimism; and 4) when facing a failure, imagining how things could have been worse and taking control of the situation.[160]

In an experiment, people who considered themselves exceptionally lucky or unlucky were asked to count the number of photographs in a newspaper. On average, those who considered themselves unlucky spent two minutes counting, while the self-claimed lucky had the right answer in a few seconds.

How could that happen? Well, on the second page of the newspaper there was a headline in 5-cm-high font: *"Stop counting. There are 43 photographs in this newspaper."* It wasn't luck—it was seeing the bigger picture and watching for opportunities. People who blame external factors are more prone to miss opportunities.

The feeling of having bad luck impedes your results. It also causes you to blame others, or other circumstances. And blame throwing has been proven to be socially contagious. When you attribute a personal failure to another person or event, that negativity tends to spread from one individual to another. In the end it'll return to you as blame from others.[161]

The desire to blame other people or external factors is sometimes caused by focusing on goals that are too distant in the future. You forget to work here and now, given the facts that exist. Recognizing your real options helps you to get more control over your decisions, gain more information when you have to decide, and stop making the wrong decisions.[162]

RELATIONSHIP RESPONSIBILITY

I've seen many personal conflicts during my twenty-five years as a consultant in the software development industry. Peter Drucker argues that most people—even when they try—fail to understand their coworkers as well as fail to take responsibility for communicating with them.[163]

The first thing is to understand that people in your office are as much individuals as you are. You must learn what strengths and weaknesses they have. They all have their own ways of getting things done. Find the most effective way for you to cooperate with these individuals.

Even though Angela and Babak worked at desks right next to each other, they didn't get along. All sorts of accusations were always flying through the air. Their manager sent them together to a quite tough leadership course, where everybody had to open up. It worked wonders.

The second element is to take responsibility for communicating with your coworkers. Why were the other people hired by your employer? What outcomes are the coworkers looking for? What are their missions? Go ahead and ask them. Otherwise you won't understand their intentions.

My client Marie claimed she couldn't get along with her manager. After some discussion about her situation, she decided to make a bet with herself. Every time she was frustrated with his inability to make a decision she was satisfied with, she kindly and curiously asked him to explain his objectives. Empathy grew in both directions.

EFFECTIVE LISTENING

Are you an effective listener? If you answer yes, then you're a member of the majority that believe they are. A big cross-business survey revealed that almost all respondents thought they communicated as or more effectively than their co-workers.[164] But everybody can't possibly be better than everybody else.

The ability to listen effectively leads to win-win solutions. Not only does it build trust and commitment, but our decisions will also be more accurate when we truly understand the points our colleagues are trying to make. And if they happen to be wrong, we can only convince them of our own point of view when we know what theirs is.

Effective listening starts with focusing on what the other person is saying, not on forging your next reply. It requires willpower to not cut off your colleague when you know he's wrong. However, if you let him finish speaking, you may discover that you got him wrong. This abundance mentality also fosters feelings of respect and mutual support.

Reflecting and probing is the next level of effective listening. Asking reflective questions is a way of summarizing what you heard in your own words.[165] Probing is asking for more information in a non-judgmental way. Now you're probably helping your colleague think, as well.

Finally, when your co-worker's message is clear to you, try to steer the conversation to the more productive deliberative tense. Look together into the future. Instead of arguing over values or past events, explore together what the real options are now.

DELIBERATIVE RHETORIC

Although Amira knew that changing storage space providers right now would only lead to more concerns than benefits, her boss was insistent. He said that the current provider had cheated when they calculated the size of the space the company was using.

Aristotle defined three forms of rhetoric more than 2,000 years ago, each relating to a specific tense: past, present, and future.[166] The form of rhetoric in which you blame is called forensic. It's concerned with the past: Did the provider cheat or not? It often boils down to guilt and rarely contributes to good decisions.

Epideictic is Aristotle's second type of rhetoric and is concerned with the present. The present is about values rather than blame. Amira's boss told her that she was being naive because she believed the old provider would shape up its services. Is she naive or not? Is labeling her important?

Finally, Aristotle defined *deliberative rhetoric*. This type of rhetoric looks into the future, asking about the real options available. Maybe the competing provider is much more expensive than the current provider. Perhaps the cheating incident can give Amira's company negotiating power in a new contract.

If you find yourself a victim of colleagues impeding good decisions with forensic and epideictic rhetoric, reposition the conversation to future choices.[167] Regardless of who did what and how we came here, what is the best step to take right now? This leads to constructive decision making.

THE BEN FRANKLIN EFFECT

When you perform a favor for someone, it increases the likelihood that you'll be happy to do that person another favor in the future. This effect may be even stronger than the keenness to repay a favor. Your brain interprets that person's request for a favor as admiration and respect for you.

Benjamin Franklin took advantage of this effect back in 1737. In an astute maneuver, he asked a rival Pennsylvania legislator to lend him a rare book. When they next met, the former rival spoke to Franklin for the first time and with great civility. They became friends ever after.[168]

The effect was further verified in 1969. Winners of an intellectual contest were asked to either return their prize money to the cash-strapped researcher, return it to the department, or keep it. When they were later surveyed, those who were asked to give the money to the researcher rated him highest.[169]

When someone observes his own behavior, his brain wants it to make sense: *"I did someone a favor and don't really know why. Then I must have done it because I like him."* We subconsciously eliminate the cognitive dissonance between negative attitude and doing a favor.

Let's say that a colleague or stakeholder seems to refuse every idea you propose. Identify his expert area and ask him for advice on a problem that connects his area of expertise with your interests. This favor, not repaid, will make him more sympathetic towards you from then on.

COMMUNICATION BANDWIDTH

Your task is on hold because you need some information from a colleague in order to continue. You send an email requesting the info and get an answer the next day. Unfortunately, he misunderstood your question and gave you an answer that was totally irrelevant.

There's a hierarchy of richness in different kinds of communication. You can compare it to a stairway. Communicating at the lowest level demands the least effort but increases the risk of misunderstandings. Moving up a few steps improves your view but costs some energy.

The steps on this stairway come in the following order: 1) communicating through documents, 2) one-way directed texts, like emailing, 3) instant messaging, 4) phone calls, 5) video conferences, 6) face-to-face meetings, and 7) face-to-face meetings with a whiteboard or other option for drawing.

In addition to selecting an appropriate communication channel, it's also important to use the communication channel effectively. Before sending an email, analyze what information you're really looking for. Put that as a question in the subject field. Add only the necessary clarification or background information in the email body.

A full 69 percent of respondents in an HBR survey said that face-to-face communication is the best way to understand customers.[170] However, we have to balance better understanding against spending more time and effort higher up the stairs. The best strategy is to communicate at the lowest stair step that doesn't allow misunderstandings.

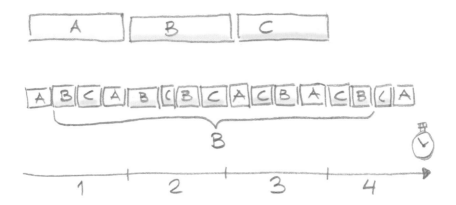

QUESTION QUEUE TIME

"All we are doing is looking at the timeline," said lean manufacturing mastermind Taiichi Ohno, *"from the moment the customer gives us an order to the point when we collect the cash. And we are reducing that timeline by removing the non-value-added wastes."*[171]

You can apply this to your own production timelines. Say you send an email to the data mining guys at your company requesting some statistics to complete the report you're working on. Two days later they respond, but unfortunately, they've misinterpreted your request. You have to email them again. And wait two more days.

Question queue time is the time we spend waiting for an answer to a blocking question. It's frustrating, it creates unfinished work-inventory costs, and it urges us to keep too many balls in the air while waiting. This last one in particular leads to task switching and inefficiency.

Assume you have the three tasks, A, B, and C. Each demands one week if you can work on it continuously. Altogether, the three tasks will take three weeks, and on average the lead time is 1.5 weeks. If you're task switching, I bet they'll take four weeks altogether and 3.5 in lead time.[172]

Don't use it as an excuse for procrastination when you can no longer influence the progress of your task. Establish communication early with those who have the knowledge you need. Don't accept several days' response time for crucial questions. Call the person, or even better talk face to face if possible.

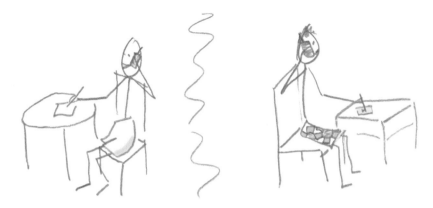

PHONE CALLS

Some tasks have a duration that you can't control. Making a business call cannot, of course, be divided into timeboxes. Telling the other person that you have to hang up because your panorama cue went off isn't very constructive or polite.

Indivisible tasks like phone calls must be separated from preparatory work and subsequent work. Before making a phone call, you should make sure you are comfortably seated and have access to pen, a paper, and your calendar. The most important preparation, though, is to jot down the purpose of the phone call.

The purpose of a call is always to get some kind of information. Even when you're the informer, you're looking for signs that the person you're calling understands and accepts your message. Write down one to three outstanding questions before you call. These represent the purpose of your call.

Be focused on your purpose. Don't spend too much time on small talk just because you're nervous about how the person you're calling will react to your purpose. Make notes during the call. Answers to your outstanding questions, tasks that either of you commits to, and appointments that you schedule must be written down instantly.

Keep the conversation short. Summarize the conversation and terminate the call politely as soon as you've got the information you were looking for. Immediately after, put any commitments in your *grass catcher list* and appointments in your calendar.

COCKTAIL PARTY PROBLEM

Our concentration on one speaker is effectively disturbed when we hear subjectively important messages in another conversation. For instance, if your office landscape neighbor mentions your name in a conversation with someone else, you will start listening to discover why they're talking about you.

Through direct recording of brain activity, researchers have shown that the parts of the brain that process raw auditory information capture both the speaker on which you are focusing as well as the speaker you are trying to ignore. But in the parts that process language, the ignored voice isn't noticeable.[173]

Colin Cherry coined the term the *cocktail party problem* to describe the human ability to focus on one person talking while shadowing all other conversations in the same room.[174] The bad habit of overhearing is more detrimental to those with limited working memory capacity.[175]

Research also shows that those who rarely multitask are more effective at volitionally allocating their attention in the face of distractions. Multitaskers do worse in this test even though they might think that they will do better than a monotasker.[176]

Effective conversations take place in an environment where only one person speaks at a time. When a discussion requires reflection and analysis appears, book a meeting. Arrange this meeting where no other interesting discussion is going on. Why not take a walk together?

DESIGNING MEETINGS

Way too many meetings demand high effort with low return[177] just because proper preparations weren't made for the meeting. The first thing to do is to decide whether the meeting is a workshop, a decision meeting, or a debriefing. This needs to be communicated in the meeting invitation.

Never have more than one purpose for a meeting. One outstanding question must be answered. Inviting more than five people to a workshop or a decision meeting hints that there are multiple purposes and thus people will have to idle until their subject is discussed.

Decision meetings should never take more than fifteen minutes, often less. If they demand more, then you either have multiple purposes that may not involve everyone invited to the meeting or it's a combination of workshop and decision meeting. That means that you didn't prepare the decision basis before the meeting.

Workshops are meetings for preparing the basis for decision making. They may last for hours and still be productive if you have frequent breaks. At least once an hour, you need to stretch your legs and oxygenate your brain for ten minutes. Set an alarm and stop instantly when it goes off.

The environment is also important for meeting productivity. Don't invite people to a room with a large conference table. Decision meetings are best performed standing up.[178] Workshop creativity benefits from holding the meeting in a café, or even better, during an outdoor walk.[179]

INVITATION ACCEPTANCE CRITERIA

If you have too many meetings, they will starve out your discretionary time. Not only do you spend time in meetings, but you also commit to tasks in meetings that you don't have time to implement. You must find a balance while also participating in the right meetings. It's handy to have a list of acceptance criteria to consult when invitations are received.

Before accepting an invitation, you must understand whether it's a workshop, a debriefing, or a decision meeting. A meeting that is a mixture of all three is rarely effective. The participants in a decision meeting must be empowered to make decisions and have clear options prepared in advance.

What is the purpose of this meeting? What outcome is the person who initiated the meeting expecting? If there are several purposes, maybe the organizer can split the meeting into more than one meeting. If the purpose is not even described in the invitation, start by requesting such a description.

Some project managers have a bad habit of inviting multiple people to debriefing meetings. It costs the company a lot of money when participants wait for their turn to give a summary of their ongoing work. These talks are more effective one-on-one—manager and you.

Multiple purposes, too many participants, and meetings that last for too many hours all make meetings unproductive. *Parkinson's law*—that work expands to fill available time—is often present in meetings.[180] Consider that before accepting an invitation. List your acceptance criteria.

NONVERBAL COMMUNICATION

I was once in a meeting where three people repeated their arguments over and over again. The mood was tense. No one seemed to even understand anyone else's position. It was like a dialogue of the deaf. Then young Miss Petrova rose to her feet and walked to the whiteboard.

Sometimes verbal conversation doesn't work. We all have different backgrounds and experiences, which can lead to misunderstanding each other. Visual communication works particularly well for abstract ideas. Venn diagrams, line graphs, and flowcharts can help to clearly express the thing that's so hard to express verbally.

Don't try to make your diagrams cover everything and don't make them too precise. Scales should be fuzzy, if they are used at all. Precision puts the focus on the accuracy of your sketch instead of on the idea, where it belongs. When there are misunderstandings, draw a new diagram instead of correcting the first one.[181]

In the fantastic book *The Back of the Napkin*, Dan Roam explains how to rapidly present business ideas visually. The book doesn't target only artists. It's a simple process that creates easy-to-grasp solutions to who-and-what problems, how-much problems, and when problems.[182]

Young Miss Petrova grabbed a whiteboard pen and started to draw. Below each of her three diagrams, she wrote the name of one of the debaters. Everyone went quiet. Then Mr. Roland said: *"Now I understand what you mean. I agree and it doesn't even contradict my position."*

SUBSTANTIAL ESTIMATES

"We need a new IT services provider. Therefore, we must evaluate the players on this market. How long does it take to do that? Also, we need to look into whether we should customize the services we buy. We have to make a decision within two weeks."
Your boss obviously estimated your task for you.

A stakeholder claims he needs your estimates to make decisions. But what would he do if he found that early estimates provide little value? Guessing based on diffuse knowledge results in coarse estimates. Consequently, the stakeholder's date, cost, and scope predictions are arbitrary.

When early estimates are used as promises, we end up in the triple constraint trap. Even before we have enough knowledge, we lock scope, time, and cost. It tempts us to do the tasks we agreed upon first instead of focusing on those that later turn out to be the most important.

Many tasks are hard to estimate. These tasks might be quick, and they might take a long time. We don't know their size until we have completed these tasks. However, we don't have to be caught in the triple constraint trap. When we finish a sub-task, we have more knowledge.

Move from negotiation to partnership. When stakeholders ask you for a shaky estimate, suggest that you start with a subtask. Review and estimate together with the stakeholder after you've completed this subtask. Well-founded estimates improve transparency and predictability.

CHOKING

Sometimes even experienced and highly skilled people suffer from pressure in situations that seem pretty normal. In an ordinary meeting, you or a teammate may show strong negative emotions, even though you've been-there and done-this many times before.

You've read many books and newspapers in your life and thus can read without deliberately thinking about how to read. However, imagine that 10,000 people are listening when you're reading, but unfortunately the book is upside down. Now you're blocked. You can't read a word.

The reason you read more poorly than a beginner in such circumstances is that your procedural memory can't operate, and you feel pressure.[183] This phenomenon is commonly referred to as *choking*. It might lead to strong subconscious responses like anger, frustration, and stress.[184]

Just like the upside-down book disrupted your reading skills, something is prohibiting your colleague from subconsciously performing actions he has done many times before. His strong emotional response is in the way of rational reasoning and sound decision making.

Never respond emotionally to an emotional person. It'll only raise his arousal. Take a break or start a distracting conversation. When it's calmer, try to understand his goals and intentions.[185] Figure out why this particular issue is so important to him. What's at stake?

COGNITIVE DISSONANCE

My client Sarah told me that even though she worked hard for two months with an initiative, she was now on the receiving end of unfair criticism from her colleagues. They said she was not working toward the goal they had agreed on.

Our brain doesn't like to have two conflicting thoughts at the same time. It's called *cognitive dissonance*.[186] We feel discomfort when we behave in a way that is inconsistent with our self-image. Sarah sees herself as perceptive, but she knows their disapproval is correct.

When she was criticized, Sarah argued that her colleagues should have been grateful instead for all the effort she had put into this task.[187] It feels like there's a lot at stake when we're in cognitive dissonance. Instead of changing our behavior, we try to justify it by tweaking one of the dissonant cognitions.

Sarah had expected praise. Now she feared that losing this battle would weaken their confidence in her. We often overestimate the intensity and duration of our negative emotional reactions to future negative events.[188]

Sarah was quite nervous when she, on my advice, gathered her colleagues to listen to their suggestions. How could the group continue with this initiative? It proved to be a constructive meeting where Sarah and her colleagues pretty quickly agreed on the next steps.

SIMPLIFY COOPERATION – SUMMARY

Q: Why does waiting for replies to emails lead to task switching?
A: You start to write a business report but realize that you need some data to complement the text with a diagram. You send an email, but the next day, you're still waiting for a response to the request you sent to the data mining department. You're now forced to start a new task and can't complete your report.

Q: What can I do to get responses more quickly?
A: There's a hierarchy of richness in communication. The top level—face-to-face meetings with a whiteboard or other drawing utensils—may demand more effort but gives you detailed information immediately. Communication through emails or text messages might be the slowest way.

Q: But sometimes when I have meetings face to face, they're not effective either. Why?
A: Don't assign more than one important question to a meeting. Define in advance whether it's a decision meeting, a workshop, or a debriefing. If it's a decision meeting, make sure the participants are empowered to make decisions and that all options are prepared before you start.

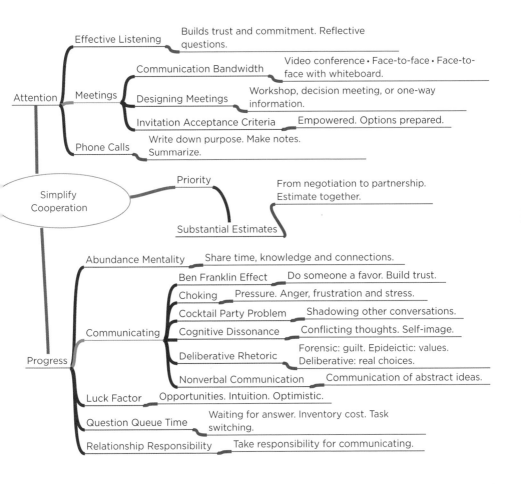

CHAPTER 7
RECHARGE CREATIVE THINKING

PRODUCTIVITY ISN'T ONLY ABOUT doing the right thing in the right way. It is equally important to prepare your mind and your body for optimum performance. Even the world's best brain fails when it is tired. What you do today can make you productive tomorrow.

Frequent breaks give airtime to our creative subconscious. Sleep, exercise, and a healthy diet helps the whole body to maintain momentum every day. Thinking with a pen in hand compensates for the limited working memory of our brain.

This chapter presents research showing how important it is to cherish our supply of energy when we want to be productive. *Eureka breaks* and *memory encoding in REM* explain how we can become even more creative.

IN ONE MINUTE: HOW TO RECHARGE CREATIVE THINKING

Five simple concepts:

- **Frequent breaks** not only give your brain a breather but will also start your creative subconscious thinking. When you return from the break, you'll often have some great new ideas.
- **Oxygenated brain** is what we get when we take a walk or exercise. Research has shown that adults who average 150 minutes of physical activity per week are less likely to feel sleepy during the day or to experience problems concentrating.[189]
- **Healthy diet** affects our thinking, creativity, and ability to remember correctly. Food that releases glucose quickly gives us energy spikes followed by drops. Fruits, vegetables, whole grains, and a healthy amount of protein provide a steadier supply of brain fuel.
- **Sleeping enough** is a proven strategy to be more productive and make fewer errors. Insufficient sleep may also mean that you miss out on the rapid eye movement sessions during which you encode, remove, and sort new memories.
- **Thinking with a pencil in your hand**[190] compensates for our extremely limited working memory. Our brain isn't wired to think about two things simultaneously and our prospective memory will benefit from written notes.

Questionnaire:

In order to kickstart your neurons, put a checkmark next to every statement below that you consider to be a recurring time robber in your current workplace.

- ☐ Three-hour meetings without breaks
- ☐ Lunch
- ☐ Poor physical fitness
- ☐ Coffee breaks
- ☐ Socializing
- ☐ Unscheduled meeting
- ☐ Noisy colleagues
- ☐ Skipped lunches
- ☐ Lack of exercise facilities
- ☐ Unfocused meetings
- ☐ Smart-phone notifications

- ☐ Business trips
- ☐ Desire for perfection
- ☐ Lazy colleagues
- ☐ Lack of sleep
- ☐ Late meetings
- ☐ Poor video conference facilities
- ☐ Unhealthy snacks available
- ☐ Working Saturdays
- ☐ Junk food in lunch restaurant

A CUCUMBER AND AN ARTICHOKE
MEET AT A VEGETARIAN RESTAURANT

Cucumber: Howdy! Everything fine, Artie?

Artichoke: A lot is happening right now. My energy is getting low. Today I almost fell asleep during a meeting.

Cucumber: Did you work late last night?

Artichoke: I left the office at midnight. The same thing happened this Monday.

Cucumber: You can't skip sleep.

Artichoke: No, it's a downward spiral. The later I work in the evenings, the worse I perform the next day. The consequence is that I stay late that day, too, to compensate.

Cucumber: Do you exercise?

Artichoke: I used to jog during my lunch break. But then I didn't eat anything, so I got hungry and snacked throughout the afternoon. It didn't really increase my energy.

Cucumber: Try to walk up the stairs instead of taking the elevator. It goes just as quickly, and it'll oxygenate your brain.

Artichoke: Good idea.

Cucumber: Another thing I usually do is park the car a mile away from the office and then walk the remaining distance.

Artichoke: I'll try that as well. One mile to the office and one mile back when I leave will do wonders for me.

THE DOWNWARD SPIRAL OF LONG HOURS

There's an old story about a naive child who asks his mother why daddy brings home a briefcase full of papers every evening. Mom explains that daddy has so much to do, he can't finish all his work at the office. The child then suggests that they must put dad in a slower group.[191]

Caroline Bird and Thomas Yutzy asked the rhetorical question: *"When will we judge work by results achieved instead of time spent?"* Some people may be more valuable working less than forty hours a week.[192] The value of a completed task isn't equal to the time you've spent on it.

Research clearly shows that the stress of overworking weakens digestion and suppresses the immune functions.[193] The extra hours today create a health debt tomorrow. Too much focus can actually impair performance on creative problem-solving tasks.[194]

Alec Mackenzie said it's a myth that the harder one works, the more he gets done. Intense activity is frequently a reaction to insecurity. It's like the French cavalry motto: *When in doubt—gallop!*[195] The ninth work hour of the day is often less productive than the first one.

In extreme cases, overtime may contribute something valuable. But you can be quite sure you'll have to pay back the same amount plus interest in the future. Poor health and lower productivity is at stake when you work long hours continuously.

TROXLER'S FADING

Swiss physician Ignaz Paul Vital Troxler discovered an optical illusion in 1804.[196] Try to stare at the little ring in the center of the picture above. First, you'll see the surrounding grey parentheses in the periphery. After a few seconds of fixating on the smaller inner dot, the parentheses disappear.

Our brain is wired to stop paying attention when things don't change, like in the experiment above. Interestingly, this is an argument for taking frequent breaks. The neurons get bored when we focus for too long on the same brain-challenging task. Our minds start to wander.

In a study conducted by Alejandro Lleras and Atsunori Ariga, subjects focused on a repetitive computerized task for forty minutes. They were also instructed to press a button if any of four given numbers were presented on the computer screen. The latter is a memory task.

In one group, the numbers didn't show up until the forty-minute session had almost ended. This group showed a significant decline in performance of the repetitive task. The other group was shown numbers on the screen intermittently throughout the task time. Their performance was unimpaired by time.[197]

Lleras and Ariga proposed that the cognitive control system cannot maintain focus on the same active goal over a prolonged period of time. Faced with long tasks, imposing brief breaks gives your brain variation. These breaks will help you stay focused.

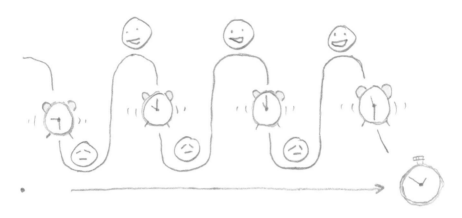

BASIC REST–ACTIVITY CYCLE

Monotasking is about doing the most important task and focusing only on that single task. Humans are not like machines that can operate at the same speed and with the same quality continuously for long periods. We perform best in cycles of energy, interspersing bursts of work with deep rests.

Nathaniel Kleitman, who discovered the phases of rapid eye movement during sleep and connected these to dreaming,[198] believed that these energy cycles are also present in the waking state—during the daytime. We have mental energy for ninety minutes' work and then we need a rest.[199]

What Kleitman called the *basic rest–activity cycle* (BRAC) is similar to what K. Anders Ericsson discovered three decades later. Many of the world's most successful athletes, musicians, and writers practice deliberately in ninety-minute sessions and take long breaks in between.[200]

Sugar and caffeine can override these natural cycles by filling our bodies with stress hormones, which are designed to handle emergencies.[201] We may be able to prolong our attention span in this way for a time. But, with the brain in fight-or-flight mode, our problem-solving capacity will decline.

I believe the world is too complex for the existence of one magical optimal focus session length number, like ninety or twenty-five. However, in my experience, it's not possible to keep a sustainable pace without frequent breaks during which we totally disconnect from the task. Breaks are mandatory.

SEDENTARY DESOLATION AND DANGER

Scottish epidemiologist Jerry Morris was looking for causes of heart attacks. In a 1953 study, he showed that the health of people in two different professions, but the same socioeconomic status, differed. Bus drivers in London were twice as likely to suffer from a heart attack compared to the conductors.[202] Think about the connection between being a conductor and spending time walking or standing.

It doesn't help to exercise intensively once a week. Sedentariness is a problem in itself. Sitting for prolonged periods increases risk for heart disease, diabetes, and cancer. It's not enough to stand up. Muscles must be used.[203] You need to take a walk in the office or do squats.

Carry a pedometer. Every time you take a break, write down how many steps you took during the break. At the end of the day you'll have a list of numbers for every break. Sum up your steps for the day. Continue like this and then compare each day's figures with your historical average.

A short walk is also a great time to clear your thoughts and let your subconscious mind come up with creative new solutions to the tasks you are struggling with. The brain is oxygenated, and you'll return to your desk healthier, livelier, and with new ideas.

Adjustable standing workstations have also been proven to increase productivity. It is not important exactly how many hours you stand up. It's the act of switching between sitting and standing that matters. After a month in a stand-capable office, productivity increases are consistent.[204]

OXYGENATED BRAIN

Physical exercise doesn't only improve our physical health, it also bolsters cognitive functions and lowers the risk for age-related cognitive decline.[205] Numerous studies also show that physically active kids perform better in school.[206]

There are many positive effects of exercising. One is to sleep better. Findings showed that adults who had 150 minutes physical activity per week were less likely to feel sleepy during the day and experience problems concentrating.[207]

Exercising increases blood pressure and blood flow everywhere in the body, including the brain. More blood in the brain means more oxygen. Oxygen is fuel for our brain. That is why exercising makes our brain perform better.

As icing on the cake, clearing your mind from conscious thoughts also starts the creative background thinking. Unscientifically, but in my personal experience, a fifteen-minute walk in the middle of the day does wonders for getting new solutions to tricky problems.

My experience is actually somewhat supported by scientific studies. For example, people who took a word association and skill test performed better if they first went on a two-day hike, compared to those who took the test before they went hiking.[208] More on this in the next section, **Creative Walk**.

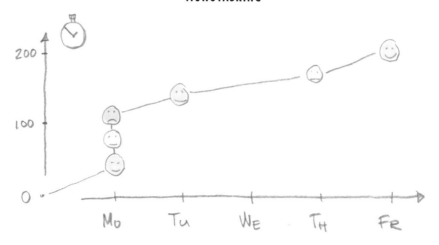

CREATIVE WALK

It feels like a creativity breakdown. What a week ago seemed like a straightforward task has proven to be a thousand loose ends without structure. Stakeholders are eagerly awaiting your end product. The simple and robust solution is to take a walk, preferably in nature.

Walking outdoors in a non-urban environment is stimulating.[209] There's a larger number of stimuli outdoors, like smells, trees, unknown people, birds, and wind. Discovering new routes is also recommended, and the more complex the path, the better.[210]

Participants in an experiment conducted a creativity test twice, in some combination of sitting or walking. The groups who walked during the first test scored best, and those who sat all the time scored worst. The group who first sat and then walked improved in the second test.[211]

Taking a walk may even have a double impact when we're in a bad mood. Several studies suggest that sedentary behavior reduces positive emotions.[212] There is also evidence that exercising can significantly increase positive mood.[213]

Visualizing can help you remember to take regular walks. Attach a diagram to your cubicle wall with weekdays on the x-axis and this week's cumulative number of minutes walked on the y-axis. To make it simple, update it by hand with a pen after each walk session. Also add a mood emoticon to show how you felt after the walk.

DERAILING LUNCH

An effective way to harm our productivity is to eat candy and pastries and drink soda all day. It causes severe spikes and drops in blood sugar levels. This gets even worse when we add a lunch of high-caloric foods such as burgers and fries. The lunch coma makes us sleepy and slow in the afternoon.

A study of more than twenty thousand American workers found that those who ate healthy food during the work day were 25 percent more likely to have higher job performance. Simply eating fruits and vegetables five times in the last week made them 20 percent more likely to be productive.[214]

One survey even showed that those who ate many fruits and vegetables during the day were happier, more engaged, and more creative.[215] When you eat more healthy snacks, you don't risk running out of brain power before lunch time even comes around.

Unfortunately, we don't make the best decisions when the brain's energy levels are low, after they've already dropped. Making choices when we're hungry makes us prefer the chocolate cake over the fruit salad.[216] To counteract this, consider making your lunch plans in the morning, when you're rested, and your brain is at full capacity.

A stable glucose level helps us control our attention, regulate emotions, cope with stress, and resist impulsivity.[217] Always keep some fruit on your desk. You will notice that it reduces your spontaneous need for both coffee and unhealthy snacks.

EXTENDED WORK PARADOX

Can your employer or customers contact you every night and weekend? We used to think that being connected to our work all the time would make us more productive. If "always on" leads to lower productivity during regular working hours, then we have deceived ourselves, haven't we? We have the technology to be accessible twenty-four hours a day, but is it clever to use it?

Jan Dettmers and his research colleagues identified two factors that influence successful recovery from work. First, we need clear boundaries between work and leisure. Second, we should be empowered to be wherever and do whatever we want in our free time.

Dettmers's study measured stress by comparing cortisol levels in participants' saliva during two very different weeks. As you might guess, participants' stress levels in the morning were higher during the week when they had to be available throughout the evening, and stress was lower when participants' evenings were truly leisure time.[218]

Note that there is a difference between flexible work hours and always being available when fires suddenly flare up. The sense of control conferred by flexible hours or telecommuting is sometimes beneficial.[219] But if you're not able to really get away, like going on an all-day picnic, in your free time, it will create stress.

There are certainly situations when you have to be available even after working hours. However, you should ensure that if you're accessible one night or weekend, then you're allowed to turn off your phone another night. *Notification celibacy* permits true recovery.

SOCIAL ENERGIZING

While the brain represents only two percent of the weight of an adult, it accounts for up to 20 percent of the body's energy expenditure. Can we minimize the energy our brain demands by working and resting in solitude? Probably not.

Imagine that the brain at rest has a baseline activity level—also called the default mode—that is restricted to certain regions of the brain. Additional activity would then show up as the tip of an iceberg when you're faced with a goal-oriented activity. It's unfortunately not that simple.

In an experiment, married women were either alone, holding a stranger's hand, or holding their spouse's hand. When warned that they were about to receive a light electric shock, the women's brain activity increased more if they were alone or with the stranger, than when they held their spouse's hand.[220]

Evolution taught our brains that we have to solve all problems ourselves when we're alone. But we also rely on the idea that cooperation with those we know will help us. We can thus relax and reduce brain energy consumption.

So maybe you should call a friend when you take a break. Or why not have a cup of coffee with your office mates? Brain power will be needed when you start again after the break.

EUREKA BREAKS

"Eureka! Eureka! I found it!" The ancient Greek scholar Archimedes howled the famous interjection repeatedly when he leapt out of his bathtub and ran through the streets of Syracuse naked. In a sudden insight, he had realized how to measure the volume of irregular objects!

You have an abstract idea about how to solve a problem but can't see the goal clearly. Maybe your idea is a dead end. You must get this idea away from your mind and inhibit it from coming back. Removing this idea will create space for other types of solutions. This is how creative thinking works.

The state of *impasse* is when one thought blocks the investigation of unexplored solutions. Computer simulations suggest that such an impasse is triggered when you associate the problem with many diverse memories.[221] There are so many ways to go, that the brain only manages to try the shortest.[222]

Trying to avoid an impasse by thinking harder is the wrong strategy.[223] Whitney Houston's face is on your mind when your friend hums *"I Will Always Love You."* But the only name you can think of is Mariah Carey. You know it's not Carey, but her name keeps blocking your thoughts.

First, we must learn to recognize an impasse. Once we have attacked a problem for a while without success, we need to back out. Take a walk in the park or get a second opinion from a colleague. Our subconscious can then launch solutions further afield in the memory.

MEMORY ENCODING IN REM

Sleep can be divided into two broad types: rapid eye movement (REM) and non-rapid eye movement (NREM). We complete between four and six cycles in a normal night of sleep. Each cycle starts with NREM, followed by REM. One NREM-REM period is approximately ninety minutes.

REM is when we dream. The brain sorts and archives impressions from our day. Unlike NREM, brain energy consumption during REM sleep equals or exceeds our brain's waking energy consumption.[224] The right and left hemispheres of the brain communicate more with each other in REM sleep.

The first REM stage in a night lasts for a few minutes. Then they become progressively longer. The last one in the morning can be an hour long. During REM, our muscles are motionless. Breathing and blood pressure both rise. And of course, REM is characterized by rapid (and random) movement of the eyes.

Encoding of a memory is the first step in a long and complex process of memory evolution that appears to be dependent on sleep. Some memories are retained, and others are forgotten. Old and new memories are combined and stored as new knowledge.[225]

This integration of memories and knowledge during REM can give us new insights. REM also supports our prospective memory and removes uninteresting noise we perceived during the day. If we shorten our sleep to six hours or less per night, we'll lose the longest REM sessions. Without REM, we'll be forgetful and stupid.

SLEEPINESS ERRORS

The National Highway Traffic Safety Administration (NHTSA) estimates that more than one hundred thousand people annually are killed or injured in the United States in sleep- or drowsiness-related traffic crashes.[226] Sleeping is not just a daily phase of inactivity. It's a key factor for being productive. Sleep gives us energy and it organizes our memories.

The effects of sleep deprivation have been compared with those of alcohol. One scientific study noted that after seventeen to nineteen consecutive hours awake, performance levels are low enough to be accepted in many countries as incompatible with safe driving.[227]

Sleep deprivation has also been shown to impair your ability to interpret new information.[228] This will naturally have a negative impact on your decision-making capacity. When you don't deeply understand what people are saying, you can't take their reasoning into account.

Some research results also suggest that sleep deprivation leads to an increased tendency to abandon rules and adopt a more fluid and exploratory approach to the environment.[229] To summarize: When we lack sleep, we act like drunks, make bad decisions, and ignore rules.

An easy way to be the best you can be in the office tomorrow is to go to bed early enough to ensure a reasonable night's sleep. Count backwards. What time do you need to get up the next morning? Subtract eight hours from that and make sure you're in bed by that time.

DISCIPLINE

Are productive people more disciplined than others? Maybe not. But if they're not, how can they be so consistent? Gary Keller gives you some hints in his best-seller *The One Thing*.[230]

Keller tells us that when we discipline ourselves for long enough, it becomes a routine—in other words, a habit. People who look disciplined have actually trained a few habits into their lives. They are not necessarily special in terms of having self-discipline. Anyone can train themselves to be disciplined, one habit at a time.

This idea goes back to what Aristotle said more than two millennia ago: *"Excellence is an art won by training and habituation: we do not act rightly because we have virtue or excellence, but we rather have those because we have acted rightly; we are what we repeatedly do. Excellence, then, is not an act but a habit."*[231]

What if you notice that you don't stick to the habits you are aiming for? Instead of accusing yourself of not being disciplined, you should take smaller steps. For example, perhaps despite your effort on the *inbox zero* habit, you still have loads of messages in your inbox. Replace your goal with something that is easier to pull off.

Also, remember that it takes time to build a solid habit. Some experts claim that it takes at least twenty-one days[232] to form a habit and others believe that on average it takes sixty-six days.[233] Naturally, it depends on what kind of behavior you're trying to learn and how far away from your current habits it is.

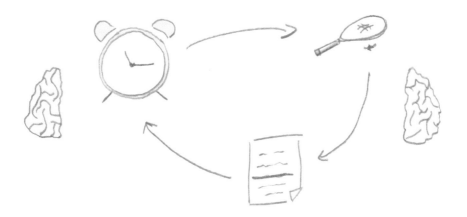

THE NEUROSCIENCE OF HABITS

Habits are like tracks worn into certain pathways in the brain. The good news is that you can design and encode your own habits. After working according to the monotasking method for a few weeks, it will become second nature. All your energy can then be focused on solving the most important task.

When we have a new kind of experience, we create new synaptic connections in the brain. If we experience the same thing repeatedly, we strengthen that connection. The part of the brain that encodes and keeps track of habits is called the basal ganglia.[234]

Our brains become more effective when they have encoded habits. Every time we experience a specific cue—for example, to set the alarm for the next *monotasking session*—we go into habit mode. Intentional activity in the cerebral cortex can be replaced with automatic procedures in the basal ganglia.

Think of it as a loop. First, a cue: you set the alarm. Then, a procedure: you focus on a single task. Finally, a reward: the alarm rings and you can cross out completed tasks.[235]

Here's the best part: After repeating the loop a number of times, we can feel the reward at the same time as our cue, without even carrying out the procedure. We already begin to feel the happiness of striking off tasks when we set the alarm for our *monotasking session*.

LASTING HABITS

Forming a habit should be fun. The sweet spot is where encouragement triggers intersect with productivity triggers.[236] Identify aspects of your life where you want change to happen. Think of easily implemented behaviors. Know the benefits and do it for yourself.

Research shows that abstract thinking is an effective method of encouraging discipline.[237] For instance, the abstract and general idea that you want to be healthier is a good target. However, the actions you implement should be small, concrete, and measurable; for instance, setting a goal to eat three pieces of fruit every day.

Use a cue to remind yourself to do the habit and don't use the old escape trick *"but first I will. . . ."* Buy the three pieces of fruit on your way to work. Eat one in the morning, one after lunch, and one at three o'clock. Do it the same way, in the same place, at the same time, every day.

Go public. Tell as many people as possible that you are trying to form your new habit.[238] This is not about putting pressure on yourself. Just explaining and arguing for your idea and its implementation will convince and remind you. You might get tips from others as well.

No need to feel embarrassed when you have a setback. Don't silently give in just because you didn't do what you planned for today. It's no big deal. The more often you do your habit, the stronger it will become. Dropping guilt makes you stronger.[239] Continue as planned tomorrow.

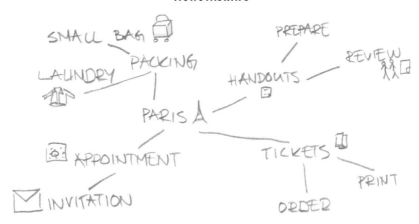

MIND MAPPING

I use *mind mapping* several times every day. Radiant thinking is often a great way to sort concepts by association instead of listing them in order. A mind map can also be helpful for analyzing a situation before taking an important decision.

Start by writing the topic in the center of a piece of paper. Drawing something next to the word helps the memory, but it isn't mandatory. Add concepts associated with the topic and connect them with a line radiating from the topic to the associated idea. Now, the topic and the associated concepts are both part of the mind map.

Mind maps have been proven to be great for aiding long-term memorization.[240] One study also showed it improves critical thinking skills.[241] The brain likes to make associations between concepts.[242] Unfortunately, sequential notes and linear thinking don't support that.

It's absolutely not important for the mind map to look beautiful. The value is in the simple and unrestricted way it allows you to record thoughts and ideas multidimensionally. Your mind map also doesn't have to be complete or perfect in any sense. Just add concepts recklessly.

If you're serious about gaining proficiency with mind mapping, then I recommend Tony Buzan's *The Mind Map Book*.[243] However, remember that mind mapping is just a tool. Similar to a hammer, you should only use it if it serves you, not in order to look professional.

RECHARGE CREATIVE THINKING – SUMMARY

Q: "Stop starting, start finishing" is a mantra in monotasking. What if I can't solve a task? Should I start a new one?

A: Sometimes we can't solve a task because of a creative *impasse*. The solution is there somewhere, but we can't reach it because another, simpler, thought is blocking our mind. Instead of multitasking with other projects, we can remove the blocking thought by taking a walk.

Q: Are there any particular walking conditions that are more successful?

A: Walking outdoors in non-urban environments has been proven to be good for our creativity. But in general, physical exercise improves our cognitive capability. And don't forget to exercise regularly; it doesn't have to take a long time. A five-minute walk inside the office every hour is better than nothing.

Q: What other lifestyle behaviors can make me more alert?

A: Without sufficient sleep, we pay a heavy price by forgetting things and making more mistakes. Blood sugar spikes and drops are devastating for our brain energy. Research shows that people who eat more fruits and vegetables are more productive.

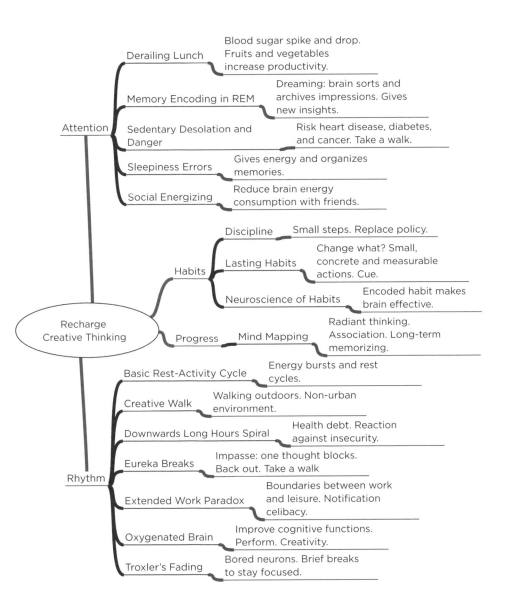

AFTERWORD

TRIGGERED BY THE SUCCESS of my book *Pomodoro Technique Illustrated*, I was invited to China. I spent October 2015 traveling around this beautiful country. I taught personal productivity in small bookshops in Tianjin and at huge conferences in Shanghai. Almost every day, I gave a speech in a new city—Shenzhen, Nanjing, Beijing. And everywhere I met curious people who asked: *"How can we complete things when we have so many tasks to do?"* The answer is monotasking—delivering the vital few by skipping the useful many.

The truth is that you won't get more done just because you accept more requests—rather, it's the other way around. And you can start today. It's simple. Write down your five most important tasks right now on a piece of paper. This is your current *short list*. Now use your intuition to pick one of these five tasks and focus on that one and on nothing else.

When you have tried monotasking for two weeks, don't hesitate to connect with me and tell me about what you experienced. You can send me an email at staffan.noteberg@rekursiv.se or you can connect with me on social media. You'll find me on WeChat, Twitter, Facebook, LinkedIn, and most other services.

I'm looking forward to learning how monotasking worked for you.
Best Regards // *Staffan*

ACKNOWLEDGMENTS

THANKS TO Erik Alsmyr, Tobias Anderberg, Karl Dickson, Åsa Dickson, Ola Ellnestam, Mats Henricson, Lina Leufvén, Viktor Nordling, Ann-Sofie Nöteberg, Joakim Ohlrogge, Tomas Rahkonen, 杨琳, and 姜丁坤.

AUTHOR BIOGRAPHY

STAFFAN NÖTEBERG is the author of the bestseller *Pomodoro Technique Illustrated*, which is translated into many languages and has sold half a million copies around the world. He has a background in the IT industry, particularly in software development. He has helped many large- and medium-sized organizations—in finance, health care, telecommunications, retail and many other industries—implement Agile and Lean. He has also taught tens of thousands of people how to improve their personal productivity. He lives in Stockholm, Sweden and Istanbul, Turkey.

INDEX

ENDNOTES

1   Marrow, A. J. *The Practical Theorist: The Life and Work of Kurt Lewin*. New York: Basic Books, 1969.

2   Zeigarnik, B. "Das Behalten erledigter und unerledigter Handlungen." *Psychologische Forschung* 9 (1927).

3   Rogers, R. D., and S. Monsell. "Costs of a Predictable Switch Between Simple Cognitive Tasks." *Journal of Experimental Psychology: General* 124, no. 2 (1995).

4   Levitin, D. J. *The Organised Mind: Thinking Straight in the Age of Information Overload*. New York: Dutton, 2014.

5   Lakein, A. *How To Get Control of Your Time and Your Life*. New American Library, 1974.

6   Biswas, A., P. I. Oh, G. E. Faulkner, et al. "Sedentary Time and Its Association With Risk for Disease Incidence, Mortality, and Hospitalization in Adults: A Systematic Review and Meta-Analysis." *Annals of Internal Medicine*, 2015.

7   "The Road To Preventing Drowsy Driving Among Shift Workers Employer Administrator's Guide." National Highway Traffic Safety Administration and National Center on Sleep Disorders Research,1998.

8   Loprinzi, Paul D., and Bradley J. Cardinal. "Association Between Objectively-Measured Physical Activity and Sleep." *Mental Health and Physical Activity* 4, no. 2 (2011).

9   Hamer M., and Y. Chida. "Physical Activity and Risk of Neurodegenerative Disease: A Systematic Review of Prospective Evidence." *Psychological Medicine* 39 (2009).

10 Atchley, R. A., D. L. Strayer, P. Atchley. "Creativity in the Wild: Improving Creative Reasoning Through Immersion in Natural Settings." *PLoS One* (December 12, 2012).

11 Oppezzo, M., D. L. Schwartz. "Give Your Ideas Some Legs: The Positive Effect of Walking on Creative Thinking." *Journal of Experimental Psychology: Learning, Memory, and Cognition* 40, no. 4 (2014).

12 Conner, T. S., K. L. Brookie, A. C. Richardson, M. A. Polak, M. A. "On Carrots and Curiosity: Eating Fruit and Vegetables is Associated with Greater Flourishing in Daily Life." *British Journal of Health Psychology* 20, no. 2 (2014).

13 Drucker, P. F. *The Practice of Management*. New York: Harper & Row, 1954.

14 Pink, D. H. *Drive: The Surprising Truth About What Motivates Us*. Riverhead Books, 2009.

15 Clear, J. "Warren Buffett's 'Two-List' Strategy: How to Maximize Your Focus and Master Your Priorities." HuffPost, December 24, 2014.

16 Eisenhower, D. D. "Address at the Second Assembly of the World Council of Churches" (speech, Evanston, IL, August 19, 1954). The American Presidency Project.

17 Hummel, C. E. *Tyranny of the Urgent*. InterVarsity Press, 1967.

18 Covey, S. R. *The 7 Habits of Highly Effective People*. New York: Simon & Schuster, 1989.

19 Hummel, C. E. *Tyranny of the Urgent*. InterVarsity Press, 1967.

20   Lakein, A. *How To Get Control of Your Time and Your Life*. New American Library, 1974.

21   Little, J. D. C. "A Proof for the Queuing Formula: L = λW." *Operations Research* 9, no. 3 (1961).

22   DeVoe S. E., and J. House. "Time, Money, and Happiness: How Does Putting a Price on Time Affect Our Ability to Smell the Roses?" *Journal of Experimental Social Psychology* 48, no. 2 (2012).

23   Ferriss T. *The 4-Hour Work Week: Escape the 9–5, Live Anywhere and Join the New Rich*. New York: Random House, 2007.

24   Kreider T. *We Learn Nothing: Essays and Cartoons*. New York: Simon and Schuster, 2012.

25   Pink, D. H. *Drive: The Surprising Truth About What Motivates Us*. Riverhead Books, 2009.

26   Hobbs, C. R. *Time Power*. Harper & Row, 1987.

27   Forster, M. *Secrets of Productive People: 50 Techniques To Get Things Done*. Teach Yourself, Hachette UK, 2015.

28   Oncken Jr, W., and D. L. Wass. "Management Time: Who's Got the Monkey?" *Harvard Business Review*, November–December Issue, 1974.

29   Benson, J., and T. DeMaria Barry. *Personal Kanban: Mapping Work, Navigating Life*. Seattle: Modus Cooperandi Press, 2011.

30   Allen, D. *Getting Things Done: The Art of Stress-Free Productivity*. New York: Viking, 2001.

31   Jackson, T. W., R. J. Dawson, and D. Wilson. "Case Study: Evaluating the Effect of Email Interruptions Within the Workplace." Conference on Empirical Assessment in Software Engineering, Keele University, April 2002.

32   Reynolds, G. *Presentation Zen: Simple Ideas on Presentation Design and Delivery*. New Riders Pub., 2008.

33   Rock, D. *Your Brain at Work: Strategies for Overcoming Distraction, Regaining Focus, and Working Smarter All Day Long* New York: Harper Collins, 2009.

34   Ibid.

35   Winston, S. *The Organized Executive: New Ways to Manage Time, Paper, and People*. Norton, 1983.

36   Dahl, M. "The Sad Truth About Speed Reading: It Doesn't Work." The Cut, April 18, 2016.

37   Rayner, K., E. R. Schotter, M. E. J. Masson, et al. "So Much to Read, So Little Time: How Do We Read, and Can Speed Reading Help?" *Psychological Science in the Public Interest* 17, no. 1 (2016).

38   McCay, J.T. *The Management of Time*. Prentice-Hall, 1959.

39   Cooper, J. D. *How To Get More Done In Less Time*. Doubleday, 1962.

40   Cobham, A. "Priority Assignment in Waiting Line Problems." *Journal of the Operations Research Society of America* 2, no. 1 (1954).

41   Little, J. D. C. "A Proof for the Queuing Formula: L = λW." *Operations Research* 9, no. 3 (1961).

42   Godin, S. *The Dip: A Little Book that Teaches You when to Quit (and when to Stick)*. Portfolio, 2007.

43   Zeigarnik, B. "Das Behalten erledigter und unerledigter Handlungen." *Psychologische Forschung* 9 (1927).

44   Gonzalez-Rivas, G., and L. Larsson. *Far from the Factory: Lean for the Information Age*. CRC Press, 2010.

45   Markovitz, D. *A Factory of One: Applying Lean Principles to Banish Waste and Improve Your Personal Performance*. CRC Press, 2011.

46   Stephens, K. S. *Juran, Quality, and a Century of Improvement*. ASQ Quality Press, 2005.

47   Clear, J. "Warren Buffett's 'Two-List' Strategy: How to Maximize Your Focus and Master Your Priorities." HuffPost, December 24, 2014.

48   Zeigarnik, B. "Das Behalten erledigter und unerledigter Handlungen." *Psychologische Forschung* 9 (1927).

ENDNOTES

49 McKeown, G. *Essentialism: The Disciplined Pursuit of Less*. New York: Random House, 2014.

50 "Laws of Thermodynamics." Wikipedia, Wikimedia Foundation, December 13, 2019.

51 Zeigarnik, B. "Das Behalten erledigter und unerledigter Handlungen." *Psychologische Forschung* 9 (1927).

52 Jackson, T. W., R. J. Dawson, and D. Wilson. "Case Study: Evaluating the Effect of Email Interruptions Within the Workplace." Conference on Empirical Assessment in Software Engineering, Keele University, April 2002.

53 Zeigarnik, B. "Das Behalten erledigter und unerledigter Handlungen." *Psychologische Forschung* 9 (1927).

54 Medina, J. *Brain Rules: 12 Principles for Surviving and Thriving at Work, Home, and School.* Seattle: Pear Press, 2008.

55 Rubinstein, J. S., D. E. Meyer, and J. E. Evans. "Executive Control of Cognitive Processes in Task Switching." *Journal of Experimental Psychology: Human Perception and Performance* 27 (2001).

56 Simon, H. A. *Administrative Behavior, 4th Edition*. Simon and Schuster, 1997.

57 Drucker, P. F. *The Effective Executive*. Heinemann. 1967.

58 Miller, G. A. "The Magical Number Seven, Plus or Minus Two: Some Limits on Our Capacity for Processing Information." *Psychological Review* 63, no. 2 (1956).

59 Cowan, N. "The Magical Number 4 in Short-Term Memory: A Reconsideration of Mental Storage Capacity." *Behavioral and Brain Sciences* 24, no. 1 (2001).

60 McElree, B. "Working Memory and Focal Attention." *Journal of Experimental Psychology: Learning, Memory, and Cognition* 27, no. 3 (2001).

61 Jackson T. W., R. J. Dawson, and D. Wilson. "The Cost of Email Interruption." *Journal of Systems and Information Technology* 5, no. 1 (2001).

62 Hobbs, C. R. *Time Power*. Harper & Row, 1987.

63 Sohlberg, M. M., and C. A. Mateer. *Introduction to Cognitive Rehabilitation: Theory and Practice.* Guilford Press, 1989.

64 Gladstones, W. H., M. A. Regan, and R. B. Lee. "Division of Attention: The Single-Channel Hypothesis Revisited." *The Quarterly Journal of Experimental Psychology Section A: Human Experimental Psychology* 41, no. 1 (1989).

65 Jersild, A. T. "Mental Set and Shift." *Archives of Psychology* 89 (1927).

66 Rubinstein, J. S., D. E. Meyer, and J. E. Evans. "Executive Control of Cognitive Processes in Task Switching." *Journal of Experimental Psychology: Human Perception and Performance* 27 (2001).

67 Just, M. A., T. A. Keller, and J. A. Cynkar. "A Decrease in Brain Activation Associated With Driving When Listening to Someone Speak." *Brain Research* 1205 (2008).

68 Jackson, T. W., R. J. Dawson, and D. Wilson. "Case Study: Evaluating the Effect of Email Interruptions Within the Workplace." Conference on Empirical Assessment in Software Engineering, Keele University, April 2002.

69 Zeigarnik, B. "Das Behalten erledigter und unerledigter Handlungen." *Psychologische Forschung* 9 (1927).

70 Stone, L. "Continuous Partial Attention: Not the Same as Multi-Tasking." *Bloomberg Businessweek* (July 24, 2008).

71 Bengtsson, C. *Konsten att fokusera: 10.9*. Volante, 2015.

72 Dismukes, R. K. "Prospective Memory in Workplace and Everyday Situations." *Current Directions in Psychological Science* 21, no. 4 (2012).

73 Loukopoulos, L. D., R. K. Dismukes, and I. Barshi. *The Multitasking Myth: Handling Complexity in Real-world Operations*. Ashgate Publishing Group, 2009.

74 Shapiro K., ed. *The Limits of Attention: Temporal Constraints in Human Information Processing.* Oxford University Press, 2001.

75   Raymond, J. E., K. L. Shapiro, and K. M. Arnell. "Temporary Suppression of Visual Processing in an RSVP Task: An Attentional Blink?" *Journal of Experimental Psychology: Human Perception and Performance* 18, no. 3 (1992).

76   Engstrom, T. W., and R. A. Mackenzie. *Managing Your Time: Practical Guidelines on the Effective Use of Time*. Zondervan Publishing House, 1967.

77   Wajcman, J., and E. Rose. "Constant Connectivity: Rethinking Interruptions at Work." *Organization Studies* 32, no. 7 (July 2011).

78   Zeigarnik, B. "Das Behalten erledigter und unerledigter Handlungen." *Psychologische Forschung* 9 (1927).

79   Fox, J. G., and E. D. Embrey. "Music—an Aid to Productivity." *Applied Ergonomics* 3, no. 4 (1972).

80   Venetjoki N., A. Kaarlela-Tuomaala, E. Keskinen, and V. Hongisto. "The Effect of Speech and Speech Intelligibility on Task Performance." *Ergonomics* 49, no.11 (2006).

81   Galván, V. V., R. S. Vessal, and M. T. Golley. "The Effects of Cell Phone Conversations on the Attention and Memory of Bystanders." *PLoS One* (March 13, 2013).

82   Brodsky, W., and Z. Slor. "Background Music as a Risk Factor for Distraction Among Young-Novice Drivers." *Accident Analysis & Prevention* 59 (2013).

83   Smith, C. A., and L. W. Morris. "Differential Effects of Stimulative and Sedative Music on Anxiety, Concentration, and Performance." *Psychological Reports* 41 (1977).

84   DeLoach, A. G., J. P. Carter, and J. Braasch. "Tuning the Cognitive Environment: Sound Masking with 'Natural' Sounds in Open-Plan Offices." *Journal of Acoustical Society of America* 137, no. 2291 (2015).

85   Dolegui, A. S. "The Impact of Listening to Music on Cognitive Performance." *Student Pulse* 5, no. 09 (2013).

86   Winston, S. *The Organized Executive: New Ways to Manage Time, Paper, and People*. Norton, 1983.

87   Zeigarnik, B. "Das Behalten erledigter und unerledigter Handlungen." *Psychologische Forschung* 9 (1927).

88   Sanders, J. *The 5 A.M. Miracle: Dominate Your Day Before Breakfast*. Ulysses Press, 2015

89   Haynes, A. B., T. G. Weiser, W. R. Berry, et al. "A Surgical Safety Checklist to Reduce Morbidity and Mortality in a Global Population." *New England Journal of Medicine* 360, no. 5 (2009).

90   Gawande, A. *The Checklist Manifesto: How to Get Things Right*. Henry Holt and Company, 2009.

91   Pauk, W. *How to Study in College*. Houghton Mifflin, 1962.

92   Bjork, R. A. "Memory and Metamemory Considerations in the Training of Human Beings." In *Metacognition: Knowing about Knowing*, edited by Metcalfe, J., and A. Shimamura. Cambridge, MA: MIT Press, 1994.

93   Mueller, P. A., and D. M. Oppenheimer. "The Pen Is Mightier Than the Keyboard: Advantages of Longhand Over Laptop Note Taking." *Psychological Science* 25, no. 6 (2014).

94   Hobbs, C. R. *Time Power*. Harper & Row, 1987.

95   Amabile, T. M., et al. "Time Pressure And Creativity In Organizations: A Longitudinal Field Study." Harvard Business School Working Paper, No. 02-073, April 2002.

96   DeDonno, M. A., and H. A. Demaree, H. A. "Perceived Time Pressure and the Iowa Gambling Task." *Judgment and Decision Making* 3, no. 8 (2008).

97   Zeigarnik, B. "Das Behalten erledigter und unerledigter Handlungen." *Psychologische Forschung* 9 (1927).

98   Ibid.

99   Ovsiankina, M. "Die Wiederaufnahme unterbrochener Handlungen." *Psychologische Forschung* 11, no. 1 (1928).

100 Zauberman, G., and J. G. Lynch Jr. "Resource Slack and Propensity to Discount Delayed Investments of Time Versus Money." *Journal of Experimental Psychology: General* 134, no. 1 (2005).

101 Shu, S. B., and A. Gneezy. "Procrastination of Enjoyable Experiences." *Journal of Marketing Research* 47, no. 5 (2010).

102 Eisenhower, D. D. "Address at the Second Assembly of the World Council of Churches" (speech, Evanston, IL, August 19, 1954). The American Presidency Project.

103 Csikszentmihályi, M. *Flow: The Psychology of Optimal Experience*. Harper & Row, 1990.

104 Jönsson, B. *Unwinding the Clock: 10 Thoughts on Our Relationship to Time*. Harcourt, 2001.

105 Zeigarnik, B. "Das Behalten erledigter und unerledigter Handlungen." *Psychologische Forschung* 9 (1927).

106 Greist-Bousquet, S., and N. Schiffman. "The Effect of Task Interruption and Closure on Perceived Duration." *Bulletin of the Psychonomic Society* 30, no. 1 (1992).

107 Johnson, P. B., A. Mehrabian, and B. Weiner. "Achievement Motivation and the Recall of Incomplete and Completed Exam Questions." *Journal of Educational Psychology* 59, no. 3 (1968).

108 Engstrom, T. W., and R. A. Mackenzie. *Managing Your Time: Practical Guidelines on the Effective Use of Time*. Zondervan Publishing House, 1967.

109 Ovsiankina, M. "Die Wiederaufnahme unterbrochener Handlungen." *Psychologische Forschung* 11, no. 1 (1928).

110 Rosenbaum, D. A., L. Gong, and C. A. Potts. "Pre-Crastination: Hastening Subgoal Completion at the Expense of Extra Physical Effort." *Psychological Science* 25, no. 7 (2014).

111 Ovsiankina, M. "Die Wiederaufnahme unterbrochener Handlungen." *Psychologische Forschung* 11, no. 1 (1928).

112 Hobbs, C. R. *Time Power*. Harper & Row, 1987.

113 Montagne P. *The Concise Larousse Gastronomique: The World's Greatest Cookery Encyclopedia*. Hamlyn, 1988.

114 Ortiz, C. A., and M. Park. *Visual Controls: Applying Visual Management to the Factory*. CRC Press, 2011.

115 Bengtsson, C. *Konsten att fokusera: 10.9*. Volante, 2015.

116 Dalton, A. N., and S. A. Spiller. "Too Much of a Good Thing: The Benefits of Implementation Intentions Depend on the Number of Goals." *Journal of Consumer Research* 39 (2012).

117 Zauberman, G., and J. G. Lynch Jr. "Resource Slack and Propensity to Discount Delayed Investments of Time Versus Money." *Journal of Experimental Psychology: General* 134, no. 1 (2005).

118 Shu, S. B., and A. Gneezy. "Procrastination of Enjoyable Experiences." *Journal of Marketing Research* 47, no. 5 (2010).

119 Gamow G. *The Great Physicists from Galileo to Einstein*. Dover Publications, 1988.

120 Ovsiankina, M. "Die Wiederaufnahme unterbrochener Handlungen." *Psychologische Forschung* 11, no. 1 (1928).

121 Zeigarnik, B. "Das Behalten erledigter und unerledigter Handlungen." *Psychologische Forschung* 9 (1927).

122 Stanovich, K. E., and R. F. West. "Individual Differences in Reasoning: Implications for the Rationality Debate?" *Behavioral and Brain Sciences* 23 (2000).

123 Kahneman, D. *Thinking, Fast and Slow*. Farrar, Straus and Giroux, 2011.

124 Vohs, K. D., J. P. Redden, and R. Rahinel. "Physical Order Produces Healthy Choices, Generosity, and Conventionality, Whereas Disorder Produces Creativity." *Psychological Science* 24, no. 9 (2013).

125   Beck, D. M., and S. Kastner. "Top-down and Bottom-up Mechanisms in Biasing Competition in the Human Brain." *Vision Research* (2008).

126   Churchman, C. W. "Wicked Problems." *Management Science* 14, no. 4 (December 1967).

127   Simon, H. A. *The Sciences of the Artificial.* M.I.T. Press, 1969.

128   Harris, A. *Creativity and Education.* Palgrave Macmillan, 2016.

129   Dunne, K. J., and E. S. Dunne. *Translation and Localization Project Management: The Art of the Possible.* John Benjamins Publishing, 2011.

130   Buzan, T., and B. Buzan. *The Mind Map Book: How to Use Radiant Thinking to Maximize Your Brain's Untapped Potential.* Dutton, 1993.

131   Cameron, J., K. M. Banko, and W. D. Pierce. "Pervasive Negative Effects of Rewards on Intrinsic Motivation: The Myth Continues." *The Behavior Analyst* 24 (2001).

132   Frankl, V.E. - *...trotzdem Ja zum Leben sagen: Ein Psychologe erlebt das Konzentrationslager.* Vienna, Autria: Verlag für Jugend und Volk, 1946.

133   Pink, D. H. *Drive: The Surprising Truth About What Motivates Us.* Riverhead Books, 2009.

134   Vohs, K. D., R. E. Baumeister, B. J. Schmeichel, et al. "Making Choices Impairs Subsequent Self-Control: A Limited-Resource Account of Decision Making, Self-Regulation, and Active Initiative." *Journal of Personality and Social Psychology* 94 (2008).

135   Sievertsen, H. H., F. Gino, and M. Piovesan. "Cognitive Fatigue Influences Students' Performance on Standardized Tests." *PNAS* 113, no. 10 (2016).

136   Blain, B., G. Hollard, and M. Pessiglione. "Neural Mechanisms Underlying the Impact of Daylong Cognitive Work on Economic Decisions." *PNAS* 113, no. 25 (2016).

137   Tracy, B. *Eat that Frog!: 21 Great Ways to Stop Procrastinating and Get More Done in Less Time.* Berrett-Koehler Publishers, 2001.

138   Zeigarnik, B. "Das Behalten erledigter und unerledigter Handlungen." *Psychologische Forschung* 9 (1927).

139   Lakein, A. *How To Get Control of Your Time and Your Life.* New American Library, 1974.

140   Ries, E. *The Lean Startup: How Today's Entrepreneurs Use Continuous Innovation to Create Radically Successful Businesses.* Crown Publishing Group, 2011.

141   Hofstadter, D. R. *Gödel, Escher, Bach: An Eternal Golden Braid.* Basic Books, 1979.

142   McConnell, S. *Software Estimation: Demystifying the Black Art.* Microsoft Press, 2006.

143   United States War Department. *The War of the Rebellion: A Compilation of the Official Records of the Union and Confederate Armies.* Series 2, Volume 7. Washington, DC: Government Printing Office, 1899.

144   Ariely, D., and K. Wertenbroch. "Procrastination, Deadlines, and Performance: Self-Control by Precommitment." *Psychological Science* 13, no. 3 (2002).

145   Festinger, L. *A Theory of Cognitive Dissonance.* Row, Peterson, 1957.

146   Mittone, L., and L. Savadori. "The Scarcity Bias." *Applied Psychology* 58, no. 3 (2009).

147   MacKenzie, R. A. *The Time Trap.* Amacom Books, 1972.

148   De Bono, E. *De Bono's Thinking Course.* Pearson Education, 2006.

149   De Bono, E. *Six Action Shoes.* HarperCollins Canada, Ltd., 1991.

150   Surowiecki, J. *The Wisdom of Crowds.* Knopf Doubleday Publishing Group, 2005.

151   Černe, M., C. G. L. Nerstad, A. Dysvik, and M. Škerlavaj. "What Goes Around Comes Around: Knowledge Hiding, Perceived Motivational Climate, and Creativity." *Academy of Management Journal* 57, no. 1 (2014).

152   Parkinson, C. N. "Parkinson's Law." *The Economist*, November 19, 1955.

153   Hogue, W. D. "What does Priority Mean?" *Business Horizons* 13(6), 1970.

154   Lakein, A. *How To Get Control of Your Time and Your Life.* New American Library, 1974.

155   Brooks, F. P. *The Mythical Man-month: Essays on Software Engineering.* Addison-Wesley Publishing Company, 1975.

156   Jönsson, B. *Tio år senare: tio tankar om tid.* Brombergs, 2009.

157   Černe, M., C. G. L. Nerstad, A. Dysvik, and M. Škerlavaj. "What Goes Around Comes Around: Knowledge Hiding, Perceived Motivational Climate, and Creativity." *Academy of Management Journal* 57, no. 1 (2014).

158   Covey, S. R. *The 7 Habits of Highly Effective People.* New York: Simon & Schuster, 1989.

159   Černe, M., C. G. L. Nerstad, A. Dysvik, and M. Škerlavaj. "What Goes Around Comes Around: Knowledge Hiding, Perceived Motivational Climate, and Creativity." *Academy of Management Journal* 57, no. 1 (2014).

160   Wiseman, R. *The Luck Factor: The Four Essential Principles.* Arrow, 2004.

161   Fast, N. J., and L. Z. Tiedens. "Blame Contagion: The Automatic Transmission of Self-serving Attributions." Journal of Experimental Social Psychology; 46, 2010.

162   Maassen, O., Matts, C., and Geary, C. *Commitment: Novel about Managing Project Risk.* Hathaway Te Brake Publications, 2016.

163   Drucker, P. F. "Managing Oneself." *Harvard Business Review*, March-April (1999).

164   Haney, W. V. *Communication and Interpersonal Relations: Text and Cases.* Irwin, 1979.

165   Rogers, C. R. *Client-centered Therapy: Its Current Practice, Implications, and Theory.* Houghton Mifflin, 1951.

166   Aristotle. *Rhetoric*, Courier Corporation, 2012.

167   Heinrichs, J. *Thank You for Arguing: What Aristotle, Lincoln, and Homer Simpson Can Teach Us about the Art of Persuasion.* Three Rivers Press, 2007.

168   Franklin, B. *The Autobiography of Benjamin Franklin.* The Project Gutenberg, 2008.

169   Jecker, J., Landy, D. "Liking a Person as a Function of Doing Him a Favour." *Human Relations* 22, no. 4 (1969).

170   "Managing Across Distance in Today's Economic Climate: The Value of Face-to-Face Communication." *Harvard Business Review*, 2009.

171   Ohno, T. *Toyota Production System: Beyond Large-Scale Production.* CRC Press, 1988.

172   Poppendieck, M., and T. Poppendieck. *Implementing Lean Software Development: From Concept to Cash.* Addison-Wesley, 2006.

173   Zion Golumbic, E. M., N. Ding, S. Bickel, et al. "Mechanisms Underlying Selective Neuronal Tracking of Attended Speech at a 'Cocktail Party.'" *Neuron* 77, no. 5 (2013).

174   Cherry, E. C. "Some Experiments on the Recognition of Speech, with One and with Two Ears." *The Journal of the Acoustical Society of America* 25, no. 5 (1953).

175   Conway, A. R. A., N. Cowan, and M. F. Bunting. "The Cocktail Party Phenomenon Revisited: The Importance of Working Memory Capacity." *Psychonomic Bulletin & Review* 8, no. 2 (2001).

176   Ophir, E., C. Nass, and A. D. Wagner. "Cognitive Control in Media Multitaskers." *PNAS* 106, no. 37 (2009).

177   Howard, J. "Clarizen Survey Says Employees in the U.S. Waste Up To 30 Percent of Work Week on Status Meetings." Clarizen, February 9, 2016.

178   Knight, A. P., and M. Baer. "Get Up, Stand Up: The Effects of a Non-Sedentary Workspace on Information Elaboration and Group Performance." *Social Psychological and Personality Science* 5, no. 8 (2014).

179   Vohs, K. D., J. P. Redden, and R. Rahinel. "Physical Order Produces Healthy Choices, Generosity, and Conventionality, Whereas Disorder Produces Creativity." *Psychological Science* 24, no. 9 (2013).

180   Parkinson, C. N. "Parkinson's Law." *The Economist*, November 19, 1955.

181   McCay, J. T. *The Management of Time.* Prentice-Hall, 1959.

182   Roam D. *The Back of the Napkin: Solving Problems and Selling Ideas with Pictures*. Portfolio, 2008

183   Beilock, S. L., and T. H. Carr. "On the Fragility of Skilled Performance: What Governs Choking Under Pressure?" *Journal of Experimental Psychology* 130, no. 4 (2001).

184   Barker, A. *How to Solve Almost Any Problem: Turning Tricky Problems Into Wise Decisions*. Pearson, 2012.

185   Goleman, D. *Emotional Intelligence: Why it Can Matter More Than IQ*. Bloomsbury, 1996.

186   Festinger, L. *A Theory of Cognitive Dissonance*. Row, Peterson, 1957.

187   Aronson E., and J. Mills. "The Effect of Severity of Initiation on Liking For a Group." *Journal of Abnormal and Social Psychology* 59 (1959).

188   Wilson, T. D., and D. T. Gilbert. "Affective Forecasting: Knowing What to Want." *Current Directions in Psychological Science* 14, no. 3 (2005).

189   Loprinzi, Paul D., and Bradley J. Cardinal. "Association Between Objectively-Measured Physical Activity and Sleep." *Mental Health and Physical Activity* 4, no. 2 (2011).

190   Hobbs, C. R. *Time Power*. Harper & Row, 1987.

191   Bliss, E. C. *Getting Things Done*. Bantam Books, 1978.

192   Bird, C., and T. D. Yutzy. "The Tyranny of Time: Results Achieved vs. Hours Spent." *Journal of Nursing Administration* 1, no. 5 (1971).

193   Marsland, A. L., S. Cohen, B. S. Rabin, and S. B. Manuck. "Associations Between Stress, Trait Negative Affect, Acute Immune Reactivity, and Antibody Response to Hepatitis B Injection in Healthy Young Adults." *Health Psychology* 20, no. 1 (2001).

194   Wiley, J., and A. F. Jarosz. "Working Memory Capacity, Attentional Focus, and Problem Solving." *Current Directions in Psychological Science* 21, no. 4 (2012).

195   MacKenzie, R. A. *The Time Trap*. Amacom Books, 1972.

196   Pessoa, L., and P. De Weerd. *Filling-In: From Perceptual Completion to Cortical Reorganization*. Oxford University Press, 2003.

197   Ariga A., and A. Lleras. "Brief and Rare Mental 'Breaks' Keep You Focused: Deactivation and Reactivation of Task Goals Preempt Vigilance Decrements." *Cognition* 118, no. 3 (2011).

198   Aserinsky, E., and N. Kleitman. "Regularly Occurring Periods of Eye Motility, and Concomitant Phenomena, During Sleep." *Science* 118, no. 3062 (1953).

199   Kleitman, N. *Sleep and Wakefulness*. University of Chicago Press, 1963.

200   Ericsson, K. A., R. T. Krampe, and C. Tesch-Römer. "The Role of Deliberate Practice in the Acquisition of Expert Performance." *Psychological Review* 100, no. 3 (1993).

201   Loehr, J., and T. Schwartz. *The Power of Full Engagement: Managing Energy, Not Time, is the Key to High Performance and Personal Renewal*. Simon and Schuster, 2003.

202   Morris, J. N., J. A. Heady, P. A. B. Raffle, et al. "Coronary Heart-Disease and Physical Activity of Work." *The Lancet* (1953).

203   Biswas, A., P. I. Oh, G. E. Faulkner, et al. "Sedentary Time and Its Association With Risk for Disease Incidence, Mortality, and Hospitalization in Adults: A Systematic Review and Meta-Analysis." *Annals of Internal Medicine*, 2015.

204   Garrett, G., M. Benden, R. Mehta, et al. "Call Center Productivity Over 6 Months Following a Standing, Desk Intervention." *IIE Transactions on Occupational Ergonomics and Human Factors* (2016).

205   Hamer M., and Y. Chida. "Physical Activity and Risk of Neurodegenerative Disease: A Systematic Review of Prospective Evidence." *Psychological Medicine* 39 (2009).

206   Castelli, D. M., C. H. Hillman, S. M. Buck, and H. E. Erwin. "Physical Fitness and Academic Achievement in Third- and Fifth-Grade Students." *Journal of Sport & Exercise Psychology* 29 (2007).

207   Loprinzi, Paul D., and Bradley J. Cardinal. "Association Between Objectively-Measured Physical Activity and Sleep." *Mental Health and Physical Activity* 4, no. 2 (2011).

208   Atchley, R. A., D. L. Strayer, and P. Atchley. "Creativity in the Wild: Improving Creative Reasoning Through Immersion in Natural Settings." *PLoS One* (December 12, 2012).

209   Hartig, T., G. W. Evans, L. D. Jamner, et al. "Tracking Restoration in Natural and Urban Field Settings." *Journal of Environmental Psychology* 23, no. 2 (2003).

210   Opipari, B. "Run to Write: How Exercise Will Make You a Better Writer." *Perspectives: Teaching Legal Research and Writing* 20 (2012): 104–8.

211   Oppezzo, M., and D. L. Schwartz. "Give Your Ideas Some Legs: The Positive Effect of Walking on Creative Thinking." *Journal of Experimental Psychology: Learning, Memory, and Cognition* 40, no. 4 (2014).

212   Hogan, C. L., L. I. Catalino, J. Mata, and B. L. Fredrickson. "Beyond Emotional Benefits: Physical Activity and Sedentary Behaviour Affect Psychosocial Resources Through Emotions." *Psychology and Health* 30, no. 3 (2015).

213   Steinberg, H., E. A. Sykes, and T. Moss. "Exercise Enhances Creativity Independently of Mood." *British Journal of Sports Medicine* 31 (1997).

214   Merrill R. M., S. G. Aldana, J. E. Pope, et al. "Self-Rated Job Performance and Absenteeism According to Employee Engagement, Health Behaviors, and Physical Health." *Journal of Occupational and Environmental Medicine* 55, no. 1 (2012).

215   Conner, T. S., K. L. Brookie, A. C. Richardson, AND M. A. Polak. "On Carrots and Curiosity: Eating Fruit and Vegetables is Associated with Greater Flourishing in Daily Life." *British Journal of Health Psychology* 20, no. 2 (2014).

216   Shiv, B., and A. Fedorikhin. "Heart and Mind in Conflict: the Interplay of Affect and Cognition in Consumer Decision Making." *Journal of Consumer Research* 26, no. 3 (1999).

217   Gailliot, M. T., and R. F. Baumeister. "The Physiology of Willpower: Linking Blood Glucose to Self-Control." *Personality and Social Psychology Review* 11, no. 4 (2007).

218   Dettmers, J., T. Vahle-Hinz, E. Bamberg, et al. "Extended Work Availability and its Relation with Start-of-Day Mood and Cortisol." *Journal of Occupational Health Psychology* 21, no. 1 (2016).

219   Gajendran, R. S., and D. A. Harrison. "The Good, the Bad, and the Unknown About Telecommuting: Meta-analysis of Psychological Mediators and Individual Consequences." *Journal of Applied Psychology* 92 (2007).

220   Coan, J. A., H. S. Schaefer, and R. J. Davidson. "Lending a Hand: Social Regulation of the Neural Response to Threat Psychological." *Science* 17, no. 12 (2006).

221   Langley, P., and R. Jones. "A Computational Model of Scientific Insight." In *The Nature of Creativity: Contemporary Psychological Perspectives*, edited by R. J. Sternberg. Cambridge University Press, 1988.

222   Jung-Beeman M., E. M. Bowden, J. Haberman, et al. "Neural Activity When People Solve Verbal Problems with Insight." *PLoS Biology* 2, no. 4 (2004).

223   Ohlsson, S. *Deep Learning: How the Mind Overrides Experience.* Cambridge University Press, 2011.

224   Hobson, J. A., E. F. Pace-Schott, and R. Stickgold. "Dreaming and the Brain: Toward a Cognitive Neuroscience of Conscious States." *Behavioral and Brain Sciences* 23, no. 6 (2000).

225   Stickgold, R., and M. P. Walker. "Sleep-Dependent Memory Triage: Evolving Generalization Through Selective Processing." *Nature Neuroscience* 16, no. 2 (2013).

226   "The Road To Preventing Drowsy Driving Among Shift Workers Employer Administrator's Guide." National Highway Traffic Safety Administration and National Center on Sleep Disorders Research,1998.

227 Williamson, A. M., and A. M. Feyer. "Moderate Sleep Deprivation Produces Impairments in Cognitive and Motor Performance Equivalent to Legally Prescribed Levels of Alcohol Intoxication." *Occupational & Environmental Medicine* 57, no. 10 (2000).

228 Ratcliff R., and H. P. A. Van Dongen. "Sleep Deprivation Affects Multiple Distinct Cognitive Processes." *Psychonomic Bulletin & Review* 16, no. 4 (2009).

229 Glass B. D., W. T. Maddox, C. Bowen, et al. "The Effects of 24-hour Sleep Deprivation on the Exploration-Exploitation Trade-off." *Biological Rhythm Research* 42, no. 2 (2011).

230 Keller, G. *The One Thing: The Surprisingly Simple Truth Behind Extraordinary Results.* Hachette UK, 2013.

231 Durant, W. *The Story of Philosophy: The Lives and Opinions of the Great Philosophers.* Pocket Books, 1976.

232 Maltz, M. *Psycho-Cybernetics: A New Way to Get More Living Out of Life.* Prentice-Hall, 1960.

233 Lally, P., C. H. M. van Jaarsveld, H. W. W. Potts, and J. Wardle. "How are Habits Formed: Modelling Habit Formation in the Real World." *European Journal of Social Psychology* 40, no. 6 (2010).

234 Brann, A. *Make Your Brain Work: How to Maximize Your Efficiency, Productivity and Effectiveness.* Kogan Page, 2013.

235 Duhigg, C. *The Power of Habit: Why We Do What We Do, and How to Change.* Random House, 2012.

236 Goldsmith, M., and M. Reiter. *Triggers: Creating Behavior That Lasts—Becoming the Person You Want to Be.* Crown Publishing Group, 2015.

237 Fujita, K., Y. Trope, N. Liberman, and M. Levin-Sagi. "Construal Levels and Self-Control." *Journal of Personality and Social Psychology* 90, no. 3 (2006).

238 Babauta, L. *The Power of Less: The Fine Art of Limiting Yourself to the Essential . . . in Business and in Life.* Hachette Books, 2009.

239 McGonigal, K. *The Willpower Instinct: How Self-Control Works, Why It Matters, and What You Can Do to Get More of It.* Avery, 2013.

240 Farrand, P., F. Hussain, and E. Hennessy. "The Efficacy of the 'Mind Map' Study Technique." *Medical Education* 36, no. 5 (2002).

241 Atay S, and Ü. Karabacak. "Care Plans Using Concept Maps and Their Effects on the Critical Thinking Dispositions of Nursing Students." *International Journal of Nursing Practice* 18 (2012).

242 Anokhin P.K. "The Forming of Natural and Artificial Intelligence." *Impact of Science on Society* 23, no. 3 (1973).

243 Buzan, T., and B. Buzan. *The Mind Map Book: How to Use Radiant Thinking to Maximize Your Brain's Untapped Potential.* Dutton, 1993.